WEETNAM

in 1

It is the end of Lisa and Alice's holiday. They are leaving the Hotel Oracle. They are leaving Greece. They are going to the airport. They are going home.

Lisa and Alice are on the airport bus. The bus is stopping at another hotel.

Some people are outside the hotel. They are going to the airport too.

Lisa and Alice help the woman with her luggage. They help her with the pushchair. They help her with her children.

Lisa and Alice are on the plane. Vera is on the plane too. She is sitting with her children.

The passengers are leaving the plane.

Lisa, Alice and Vera are in the airport. Alice is getting their luggage.

This is our last bag. Now we have everything. Now we must go to Customs.

Please – I must go to the toilet!

Vera is taking Peter to the toilet.

Vera is at Customs. A customs officer is searching her luggage. Alice hears two customs officers talking. She is surprised.

Vera comes into the café. She is holding Peter's hand.

Here we are at last! The customs officers are searching many travellers today. I'll take Helen and the pushchair now. My sister is going to meet me. She will help me with my luggage.

Suddenly, there are customs officers
and police officers in the café. One
officer is searching the pushchair.
He is looking in the frame.

14

The customs officers have the stolen painting. They are very pleased.

Vera's sister has her children. She is very pleased too.

To those not afraid to dare to believe, I salute you.

CONTENTS

ACKNOWLEDGMENTS

For the first volume of Tales From a Scarygirl, my thanks goes to two important people. To Stephan J. Myers, whose support and advice on choosing and honing these tales has been invaluable, and to Jenny-Lee Fisher, my talented friend, whose artistry has, once again, given a face to my creation.

Most importantly, however, my gratitude goes to my readers. Thank you, from the bottom of my heart, for supporting and believing in me.

INTRODUCTION

I am often asked why I write about the things I do and my answer really is, why not? The supernatural is such a fascinating, scary, disturbing, exciting and rewarding subject matter, that there is always something new to create.

Fear is the most potent of all emotions. It protects us, it stretches us and it helps us to be who we really dream to be. Fear drives us forward; it does not hold us back. Fear is to be welcomed, not shunned. Fear is to be celebrated. For, without fear, the world would be a dark and dreary place.

With Tales From a Scarygirl, I want to provoke your fear; I want to bring it to the forefront of your mind; I want to make your heart race; make your skin clammy; and make your senses go into overdrive. For, it is only then will I know I have achieved my aim – to scare the hell out of you!

As to where my stories come from, well, some are based on reality; some are based on things I have seen, things I have heard and things I have read. But, dear reader, most of all, they come from the deepest, darkest recesses of my mind, where only the bravest of all souls dare to venture.

Do you dare?

May fear protect you when the darkness comes.

1 THREE SILVER BULLETS

Three silver bullets were all he had left. Three silver bullets and a rifle. Jamie glanced through the murky window and saw that the moon had come out again. Their howls were echoing all around and he shook his head in despair. Three were never going to be enough.

He glanced at Annie, huddled in a corner, tear tracks showing on her dirt smudged face. *How on earth had they ended up here?* Jamie looked around him and took in the broken down "safe house" they had found. There were holes in the roof and the moon's beams were bathing the room in a dappled light. The floorboards were weak, if present, and they had had to balance across the beams to get to their respective hiding places. At least this would afford them some protection if they were found or, more accurately, when they were found.

Jamie glanced across the room at Luke, his best friend. Finally, he had sunken into sleep; the pain no doubt being responsible. He just couldn't keep his mouth shut. Jamie had always said Luke's mouth would get him into trouble, he just hadn't figured it would be this bad.

He shifted his weight to take the pressure off his left leg and, looking down, he saw the blood had soaked through the shirt Annie had tied around it. It was no good, they were never going to get out of here, not unless they could last until morning.

Jamie looked at his watch. Three hours until dawn. There was hope. This hope vanished as he saw movement at the edge of the woods. He grabbed his binoculars and focused on what he'd seen. There were about eight or nine of them; a pack.

The one in front raised its nose to the air and sniffed; fixing its gaze on the house. Jamie pulled back, dropping his binoculars as he did so. They hit the floor with a resonating bang.

'Shit,' he muttered and looked back out of the window, but could see nothing at the edge of the woods now. *Had they heard? Had they seen him?* Questions raced through his mind and he began to panic. Jamie's hands were clenched into fists and he could feel the bullets cutting into his palm.

Dammit! This was not what he'd had in mind when they'd agreed to this trip, but, as usual, he'd been overruled by Annie, Luke and the others - and now look at them. Now they were three. Jamie shuddered as he thought of what might have happened to the others. Ten was a safe number to come into the woods with, but not to split up.

What the hell had possessed them to split up in the first place? He glanced at Annie again and her hands were limp in her lap, a blood soaked cotton padding in her hand.

'Annie,' he whispered. 'Annie.' There was no answer. She must have fallen asleep. Jamie shifted his position again and winced as pain shot through his injured leg. He edged towards her, his back pressed against the wall. The floor creaked under his weight and a floor board splintered, the crack echoing around the room. Jamie held his breath and listened. Nothing.

'Jamie? Is that you?' She was awake.

'Annie, you must keep pressure on the wound, baby,' he whispered, her ravaged face just visible in the light from the moon.

'I know,' she said, pressing the pad into her cheek again. 'I'm just so tired and I feel kind of funny.'

'What do you mean, "funny"?' he said, alarmed. It wasn't supposed to take effect this quick. The rangers said it takes at least twenty four hours, but she had only been attacked a couple of hours ago.

'I dunno, baby, like I'm drugged or something. Things are moving in my body. I can hear the smallest things and I can smell them.'

'Smell who?' Jamie said, but Annie didn't answer.

'Smell who, Annie?' Silence. She had fallen asleep again, her wounded cheek pressed against her palm.

Hell, if she was feeling like this now, then Luke must be even worse, he thought and looked across at Luke again. He was covered in blood. His attack had been ferocious.

Luke, as usual, had been walking ahead of everyone else; challenging them to come and get him and get him they had. Two of them. They had attacked from both sides and whilst one of them had spilled his guts, the other had ripped open his throat. Jamie had never seen so much blood. They had disappeared back into the woods after this. Annie had stapled his stomach back together as best she could, but he had needed real help. It was then that the decision had been made to split up, figuring they would be harder to catch in smaller groups.

Jamie wondered if this had proved true. *Had the others managed to escape?* He and Annie had dragged Luke to their current hiding place. He was amazed that Luke was still alive. The staples were holding his guts inside, but he was still losing a great deal of blood. He needed medical help, but they had no way of getting that out here. No one would come.

Jamie continued to stare at Luke and his stomach lurched as he noticed changes in his friend's appearance.

Coarse hairs were beginning to sprout from the wounds on his body and his finger nails were starting to elongate. A crash on the floor below snapped Jamie's attention back. He edged towards the window again; his binoculars forgotten.

Looking down, he could see a mass of bodies just under the window. The snuffling and growling coming from them was sickening. It wouldn't be long now. Jamie glanced at the three bullets in his hand. He had nowhere near enough bullets. It was only a matter of time.

Maybe it was time to end it? Jamie loaded one of the bullets into his rifle. Movement to his right distracted him and he automatically raised the gun and fired. A shadow disappeared out of the room. He had missed. He had wasted a bullet.

He glanced over at Annie. She was still sleeping. He glanced over at Luke. He was gone; blood stained boards left in his wake. Panicking now, Jamie looked out of the window, in time to see Luke emerge out of the front door. At least, he assumed it was Luke. He looked like the rest of them now. He padded over to one of the others and huddled. Then they both turned and looked up at the window.

Jamie pulled back quickly, his heart pounding. He looked around the room for a way out. There was a door at the far end, behind where Luke had been lying. He edged around the walls, careful not to put too much weight on the remaining boards.

'Annie. Wake up. We have to move.' Jamie shook her until she woke up.

'Hey, Jamie, what are you doing? I just want to sleep…leave me alone….,' she said and closed her eyes again.

'Annie. Luke has changed. He's gone. We've got to move.'

'Changed? But I thought it took longer…the rangers said…the antidote…but that means I…oh, God.' She started crying.

'Come on, baby, please. Luke was hurt worse than us, which might be why. Annie, baby, please move. We need to get to that door over there.' Jamie pointed to the door, which he hoped led to the attic.

Annie started to shuffle towards it. When they got there, Jamie pulled on the handle, but it was locked.

'Shit! Move out of the way, Annie,' he said and smashed the handle repeatedly with the butt of his rifle, until it broke off.

'Quiet, Jamie, they'll hear us,' Annie said.

'They already know where we are. I don't think this will make a difference!' he snapped.

'Then what the hell are we trying to hide for?" she growled at him.

'Because we may have a chance and if we don't…' Jamie squeezed his palm around the remaining two bullets.

'If we don't, what, Jamie? We get ripped to shreds by a bunch of wolves?'

'No. I won't let it come to that. Now move.' He shoved her up the stairs into the attic. *Why hadn't he helped Luke when he had the chance? Too much of a coward?*

Jamie shouldered open the trap door at the top of the stairs and pulled Annie up through it, before slamming it shut. He looked around for something heavy to push over it and saw a wooden chest in the corner.

'Give me a hand with this, will you?' Between them, they just about managed to drag the chest over the trap door. Now there was no way in and no way out.

There were no windows in the attic, so he had no way of knowing what was going on outside. Jamie glanced at his watch. Two hours until sunrise. Two hours until they could get help. He studied his wound. It had healed up now and an angry purple scar was the only evidence of his attack. It had started. Jamie twisted the bullets in his hand; his head against the wall; his eyes closed.

'Annie? How's your face, baby?' No answer.

'Annie?' he said, more loudly, as a crash sounded behind him. Jamie spun around to see the chest shaking as the trap door was being forced open from below. The howls were echoing through the house now, the scratching and growling getting more insistent.

Shit! Two hours was too long. Two bullets weren't enough. He fumbled with the rifle, trying to load one of the bullets. His hands shook uncontrollably. The bullet slipped from his fingers and landed on the floor to his right.

Jamie scrabbled around for the lost bullet, the other firmly clasped in his left hand. The chest was almost free of the door now. Huge paws, with claws like talons, were being forced through the gap. He continued his futile search for the bullet. It was pitch dark. Still two hours to go. Not enough time.

He was frantic now and, in his haste, rushed his hand forward too quickly. Jamie felt the bullet skid away from his grasp.

'Noooooo!' he shouted into the dark. He took a deep breath to calm his nerves. Slowly and deliberately he loaded the final bullet into the rifle. The trap door flew open with a crash and one of the wolves jumped up into the attic, raising itself to its full height. The others followed. Jamie backed away, towards Annie. He had to protect her. One bullet wasn't enough.

'Annie! For God's sake answer me!'

From behind him came a deep guttural growl and Jamie whirled around. Annie stood six feet away from him. Her amber eyes were on fire. Her lips were pulled back from her gums in a snarl, revealing her razor sharp fangs. She started to move towards him, forcing him back towards the trap door and certain death.

He had no choice. He had one bullet. He had to do what he should have done an hour ago. He raised the rifle. He aimed it as best as he could at the heart. He pulled the trigger.

The force sent him flying backwards into the pack of werewolves that had been hunting them since dusk. The wolves had won. They had been warned. They hadn't listened.

Dawn was approaching fast and the rangers were readying their rescue teams to begin the search for the party that hadn't come back the previous night.

'What is it with these city kids?' said Captain Ralphs. 'It's as if they think werewolves are just a figment of our imagination. A goddam scare story that we use to get visitors.' He walked off towards the trail, leaving his team standing there looking at their feet.

'C'mon, we've got a lot of ground to cover,' he shouted over his shoulder.

'Hang on, Chief,' called Davis. 'Look.'

All four rangers turned to look towards the single track path that began the trek through the woods. Out trooped the lost party - bloody, dirty and dishevelled, but otherwise seemingly okay.

'I don't bloody believe it,' said Ralphs. 'They're alive.'

'Not all of them, Chief,' said Davis. 'It looks like one of them is missing.'

THE END

2 INNOCENCE

'Hello. What's your name?'

Emily looked up at the man, through her tears. He was smiling at her; a warm smile; a friendly smile.

'Emily,' she said, as she gulped back a sob.

'Hello, Emily, my name's Jack,' he said and extended his right hand towards her. It was a large hand; tanned and calloused, with short blunt nails. *He must work with his hands,* Emily thought. Her gaze traced the thick blue veins that criss-crossed the back of his hand, before they disappeared under the cuff of his jumper.

She extended her own small, delicate hand from within the safety of her black fur muffler. She placed it in his, feeling its roughness against her own soft skin, and shook it formerly.

'Do you mind if I sit down?'

Emily shook her head. He sat down next to her, careful to leave some space between them. *Maybe so as not to frighten me,* she thought and smiled to herself. He rubbed his hands together vigorously and turned towards her. The air was particularly cold, this November night.

'Are you all right?' he said, his voice tinged with concern.

Emily looked up into his eyes, so warm and friendly, and nodded. She wiped the remaining tears away with the back of her hand and sniffed.

'Here, use this,' Jack said, pulling a clean handkerchief out of his pocket.

'Thank you.' Emily put the handkerchief to her nose and inhaled. 'This smells nice. All clean and fresh, like the trees,' she said and smiled at him. He smiled back and glanced at his watch.

'What's the matter? Do you have to go already?' Emily said, her eyes filling with tears.

'Hey, hey, don't cry again, sweetheart. I don't have to go yet. I need to get you home first, don't I? Are you lost?'

Emily didn't answer him. She was watching the vein pulsing in the side of his neck. She reached out to touch it; to feel the blood move beneath her fingertips. Jack pulled back as though he had been scalded.

'Your hands are freezing! Put them back inside your muffler, to keep warm.'

Emily smiled at this, but did as he asked. She clasped her other hand inside the muffler. Both were ice cold, despite the warmth it provided.

'Emily, I asked you a question. Are you lost? Is that why you are crying?'

'No, Jack, I'm not lost,' she said, in a tone that belied her years.

'Then why are you here?'

'I always come here.'

'What? On your own?'

'Yes. I like to come here. It's where I meet people. It's where I help people.'

'What do you mean?'

Emily shrugged. 'People come to me; to talk. It helps them. I help them. Just like I'm helping you, Jack.'

'What do you mean, "helping me"? I'm talking to you because I'm worried about you, out here on your own, so late at night. You might get hurt.'

Emily smiled at this. She liked Jack. His kindness and his innocence set him apart from the others. Maybe she'd keep him. He would be good company.

'Where do you live? It's time I took you home.'

She didn't answer him. He sighed and slumped back against the bench. Emily shuffled across to be closer to him. She could feel the warmth radiating from his body.

'Emily, answer me. Where do you live?'

Still, she didn't answer. She wasn't listening to his voice. She was listening to his heart beating strongly in his chest.

She was listening to his blood flowing through his veins. She was tracing the veins on his hand with her tiny finger.

Jack shifted, as though dislodging an unwelcome pet and, placing his hands on her shoulders, turned her to face him.

'Emily, you should not be out here on your own, in the freezing cold, at this time of night. It's not safe. Anything could happen to you.'

'Will you walk me home then?' she said, pushing herself off the bench and holding her hand out to him.

At last, Jack thought. *What the hell was a kid her age doing in a park so late? Some people didn't deserve to be parents.* He hoped she lived close by; he needed to be back around ten, but he also wanted to give her parents a piece of his mind.

He looked down at her as she led him through the park. She was so tiny and delicate. She looked like an angel.

He was so glad he'd found her. The last thing he needed was for her to get caught up in this. Tonight was his chance to catch him. Fifteen men had gone missing here; their bodies having been discovered a couple of days later, in the bushes behind the bench she'd been sitting on.

They had been runners, walkers, dog owners, cyclists, single, married, fathers, grandfathers, teenagers. There was no real pattern, except that they were all men and that their bodies had all looked the same – grey and empty; a look of surprise evident in their eyes.

Jack looked at his watch again – nine thirty – it was going to be tight. The timing was crucial. It had to look natural.

His radio crackled to life then, making them both jump. *God, what part of "no contact" didn't they understand!*

'Yeah,' he said into the mouthpiece. He listened for a few minutes and then switched it off; to make sure they didn't disturb him again.

'What was that?' Emily said, staring up at him; her forehead creased in concern; her mouth set in a line.

'Just the station checking up on me. I'm a policeman,' he said, hoping to put her mind at rest.

Emily was not happy. She had liked Jack. Not now though; not now she knew what he was. Tears filled her eyes again. She had liked him so much, much more than the others, but he had disappointed her. He had made her sad and she didn't like to feel sad. She stopped abruptly.

'I'm tired. Will you carry me?' she stared up at him, a pout decorating her rosebud lips.

Jack stooped to pick her up and was surprised by how heavy she was. She nestled into his shoulder, her arms around his neck; twining her fingers in his hair.

'How much further?' Jack said.

'Not much. There's a way out of the park, behind

that bench up ahead.'

Jack picked up the pace and was soon wading through the long grass behind the bench.

'Wait a minute,' he said, stopping and looking around. 'We're back where we started.'

As realisation dawned, he felt a cold sweat swathe his skin and a hollow feeling appear in the pit of his stomach. He tried to drop her, but she was too quick for him. He winced as he felt her teeth puncture the delicate skin of his neck. He fought to push her away, but she was too strong for him. His neck felt like it was on fire and the pulling sensation against his flesh was becoming unbearable. He felt the delayed kick of adrenalin and pushed against her with all his strength, but to no avail. She had clamped herself to him like a limpet.

Exhausted by the effort and weakened by the loss of blood, he slumped to his knees. Emily let go of him and stepped back. Jack looked up at her, only to find her angelic features transformed into those of a monster; blood smeared across her lily-white skin.

He watched, helpless, as her delicate face returned to the angel he had met on the park bench. The angel of death. He could hear his pulse slowing; could feel his heart strain to find the strength to beat. The black and white dots started to form before his eyes and his breathing became laboured and ragged. He had no reserves left to draw on. He let the darkness embrace him.

Emily smiled to herself and returned to the bench; a little girl of four feet in height, with blonde ringlets, green eyes and un-naturally pale skin; a little girl of eight years of age, who was so much older; a little girl so full of innocence.

THE END

3 ROADKILL

Shit! Ava rolled over and looked at the clock. She'd done it this time. He'd be livid. She slipped her feet into her slippers and hurried out of the bedroom, stopping at the top of the stairs. She heard the gravel crunch as his 4x4 pulled onto the drive. Sweat broke out across her forehead and she absently rubbed her newly mended wrist.

It hadn't always been like this. When they'd met back in high school, Mike had been different. He'd showered her with presents and compliments, but that had changed when he went to college. He'd changed. The presents had stopped and the compliments had turned into abuse and finally into beatings. Ava's mother, Ruth, had begged her to leave him and she had; once. He'd hunted her down like an animal and had beaten her to within an inch of her life. He'd told her that if she ever pulled a stunt like that again, he would kill her. Ava had believed him. She still did.

She shuddered, as she remembered and caressed her swollen belly, a pang of guilt clutching at her chest.

'You saved me from the last one, didn't you?' she said.

Ava jumped as Mike opened the front door and stomped into the hall.

'Hi, sweetheart. Good day?' Ava said, her hands clasped firmly in front of her to stop them shaking.

'What's for tea?' Mike growled at her. 'It'll be dark soon. I gotta go out.' Without even looking at his wife, he marched into the kitchen. Ava followed, her heart hammering in her chest as she wracked her brain for what to say, knowing full well that it didn't really matter anyway.

'I can't smell cooking, Ava,' he said, turning and looking down his nose at her.

'I...I...I'm sorry. I was so tired when I got home from work that I... arghhh!' The blow caught her squarely across the jaw. The taste of copper filled her mouth and she leant against a chair to steady herself.

'M...M...Mike, please.' But he wasn't listening. He pulled a carving knife out of the knife block and started to advance towards her.

'If this baby's gonna make you forgetful, as well as fat 'n' lazy, then maybe you're better off without it. What d'ya say?' he said, poking at her belly with the knife. Ava whimpered as she pressed against the kitchen wall. He jabbed the knife through her clothes into her stomach and she felt the warmth as blood fanned across her pinafore.

'Well? What's it to be, bitch?' he snarled. Tears ran down her cheeks as she groped around for something to stop him. Mike brought the knife up to Ava's throat. She sucked in her breath. The blade cut into her neck, drawing more blood.

Ava reached as far as she could and clasped hold of the solid silver paperweight. She closed her eyes, thoughts of her baby filling her mind. Clenching her teeth, she smashed it on Mike's head. He slumped to the floor without a sound, the knife clattering down beside him; blood already beginning to pool around his head.

Ava yanked open the kitchen drawer looking for her car keys. 'C'mon, c'mon!' she urged her sluggish brain. 'I came in from work and I went…straight upstairs,' she finished and stumbled upstairs into her bedroom. As she grabbed her bag off the end of the bed, she heard the front door slam and an engine roar to life.

Shit! He'd woken up! Her mind reeled as she ran to the landing window, just in time to see Mike's car careering down the road. She didn't have time to mess about now. This wasn't just about her anymore. She had the baby to think of. She left the house and clambered into her car. Worried that he might come back, Ava put her foot down. She headed for Margot's, her best friend. Margot lived on the other side of town, but Mike didn't know where.

She belted along the wet roads, replaying the scene in

her mind. She was soon sobbing as the shock of what he had tried to do overwhelmed her. The rain hammered down and she threw the car around the tight bends that wound up through the woods to Margot's house.

'For God's sake,' she muttered and snapped her rear-view mirror onto "night vision" to stop the idiot behind her from blinding her with his main beam. *Some people had no consideration*, she thought as she slowed down to let the other car pass. It didn't pass; it just speeded up and headed straight for her. Ava stared in horror in her mirror as the car gained on her. She put her foot down hard on the accelerator, but she was no match for this idiot, on these wet roads. She panicked. No one knew where she was. *Why hadn't she phoned Margot before she'd left? Why?*

'Arghhh!' she screamed as the car rammed her. She jolted forward, banging her head on the steering wheel. Again and again, the car rammed her. Ava sped up, but she was struggling to keep the car on the twisty roads as it was. Then it rammed her again and she lost control. Her car spun, hit a low embankment and rolled over, slamming into a tree. Ava was knocked unconscious.

When she came to, her head was pounding and she could feel blood running down her cheek. She froze as she heard a blood-curdling howl close by. She looked up through the cracked window and found herself staring straight into the angry red eyes of a huge wolf.

Panicking, she released her seatbelt and screamed as pain shot through her leg as it caught on the steering column as she fell. She heard snarling behind her and looked around to see the wolf forcing its way through the collapsed back window. Ava yanked her leg as hard as she could and felt the flesh tear as she pulled it free. Tears pricked her eyes, but she blinked them away.

'Shit,' she muttered, her hands shaking as she rummaged around for her pepper spray. Suddenly, the glass splintered and the wolf thrust its head through the gap, but Ava was ready. She sprayed the pepper in its eyes and slammed the steering lock over its head. Not stopping to see the damage, she put her foot through the side window, wriggled through and ran as fast as she could into the cover of the trees. The pain in her head and leg overwhelmed her and she collapsed as the first waves of nausea hit her.

Ava dragged herself behind a tree and pressed her forehead against the cool bark to try and stay conscious. The silence of the woods surrounded her and she relaxed slightly. *Had she killed it?* She needed to get back to the road; to a phone box. No sooner had she pulled herself to her feet, than she heard its chilling howl again. She whirled around just in time to see the wolf lunge at her; its claws ripping through her cheek, before it disappeared back into the trees.

The wolf's howl continued to echo through the woods. Ava grabbed a fallen branch and staggered into the open, where she could see it coming. She turned in a slow circle, her heart pounding, trying to determine where the wolf was. She saw it too late. It lunged at her; its claws tearing at her belly. Blood poured from the wound and Ava collapsed to the ground, clutching her stomach, tears of pain and defeat coursing down her cheeks. She curled into a tight ball and lay there sobbing. Her baby, her baby. *Oh God, don't let the baby be dead,* she prayed. She remembered the day she'd found out she was pregnant.

'It was supposed to be a new start!' she screamed into the darkness. 'You're not going to take it away from me!' She gritted her teeth and pushed herself onto all fours.

'You're not going to beat m…arghhh!' The wolf lunged at her again, ripping her throat open with its teeth. An animal growl erupted from within her and she thrust the branch backwards into its chest. She heard the crack of ribs and it howled in pain and released her.

A gunshot cracked through the night air.

Ava pushed herself up and began to move as fast as she could towards the gunshot. As she stumbled forwards, it became harder and harder for her to stay upright. Her spine seemed to be arching, throwing her forward until she collapsed onto all fours. She bounded through the woods, but as she broke the tree line she stopped.

She couldn't see anything because of the glaring lights that were pointing directly at her. She could, however, hear the click of the bullet being loaded into the gun; she could hear the ratchet of the mechanism as it was chambered; she could smell the sweat and the fear of the men who stood around her; she could hear him, as he ran out of the trees behind her; and she could smell his blood. She had wounded him, but not fatally.

Ava's shoulders sagged as the click of the trigger sounded and the bullet whizzed through the air towards her. Her body responded as it exploded through the sternum, ripping through organs before exiting through the back. She heard the whistling of breath in that fight for life, so typical of humans.

She collapsed down next to him, spent, and she saw the fan of blood across his chest and the dried blood on his forehead.

'We got it, Sir. We killed the werewolf at last,' shouted the shooter and she dragged her gaze around to look at the deputy.

'Yes, we did,' Ava said and turned to look down at her dying husband.

THE END

4 RAVEN BRIDGE

Raven Bridge is its official name – its birth name if you will – but the residents of Copper Falls have an altogether different name for it.

Over the years, Raven Bridge has been the location of so many fatal accidents that the locals nicknamed it "Death Bridge".

The history of its "given" name dates back several centuries, to when Copper Falls Wood was a lot bigger than it is today. The wood was inhabited by many species of trees, but its most predominant occupant was the copper beech. Copper Falls Wood was home to the largest colony of copper beech trees in the country. It was these trees and the spectacular waterfall at the heart of the wood that gave the town its name.

Copper Falls Wood was also home to the largest congress of ravens found anywhere in the world and they chose, for some unknown reason, to roost in the copper beech trees. Local history has it that the noise created by these huge birds was enough to wake the dead.

In the mid 1970s, before trees and animals were seriously considered protected, the town council voted, by a very slim majority, to build a major road through the wood. It would connect Copper Falls to the nearest city, which was twenty miles away. Over the years, the road became so busy that the residents worried it would only be a matter of time before someone was killed.

After much debate, the town council voted, again by a slim majority, to build a bridge and linking roads - to take pedestrians and local traffic - leaving the main road to the bulkier traffic. The only place that could accommodate such an enterprise was the wood. Despite the many protests and demonstrations, it was decided that the lives of the human occupants of Copper Falls were worth more than those of its wilder inhabitants.

The construction crews moved in and by the time the bridge and link roads were completed, the ravens had moved out – every last one of them.

Once the construction crews had left, an eerie silence befell Copper Falls. My grandmother described it as being in the eye of the storm, as though the town was waiting for something. It was. It was waiting for the ravens to come back and occupy the remaining copper beech tress, but they never did.

In memory of their absent avian companions, the town named the bridge Raven Bridge.

It was twenty years later before the raven was seen again in Copper Falls.

At dawn, on 21st February 1994, Peter Johns, the milkman, was doing his rounds. He couldn't shake the sense that he was being watched and when he got back to the dairy, a sixth sense made him look towards Raven Bridge. Lining the full length of the stone wall, was an unkindness of ravens; silent ravens; still ravens; every set of eyes staring straight at him.

As though the breath was being sucked out of him, Peter's chest began to constrict and he gasped and fought for air. Within minutes, he sank to his knees clutching at his chest, before he slumped onto the pavement, dead.

The ravens, as one, launched themselves into the air, their raucous cries rousing the town with memories.

I saw it all.

It didn't disturb me or frighten me. I just accepted it. I had been warned. 'What goes around comes around,' my grandmother had always said.

'It's started, Grandma,' I muttered to myself as I climbed back into bed to await my alarm call.

Of course, no one saw what I saw that day; nor did anyone else see it the next time it happened, a few months later.

I was walking home from university, alone as usual, and was just coming out onto the High Street when I stopped and looked up at the bridge. Just as before, the ravens were perched, wing to wing, staring fixedly at something ahead. I turned to look and saw the university bus - the one I should have been on, but had missed - hurtling down the road.

It was travelling way too fast. I stood and watched, transfixed, as the driver fought to control the bus as it careered from one side of the road to the other, but he couldn't. The bus smashed headlong into the bridge and burst into flames.

I looked up to see the ravens launch themselves from the bridge, their cawing drowning out the screams of the townspeople as they rushed to the scene.

Thirty of the students from my university died on that bus; most of them my classmates. The driver survived. He wasn't from Copper Falls.

This became an all too regular occurrence over the next decade. Every few months someone died or was killed close to Raven Bridge; someone from the town. Every time it happened, the ravens were there. I saw them. No one connected the events; no one but me.

It started with things my grandmother had said, before she'd died, and the rest I gleaned from the local history section of the library.

History had it that the ravens carried an almost "mythical" element to them. They'd always acted as guardians of Copper Falls. Centuries ago, few people had travelled beyond the village in which they'd lived and so, when someone had approached, the ravens had launched themselves into the sky, their cacophony of calls alerting the villagers to the new arrival. This alarm system had served the village well and had prevented, on many occasions, bandits and other rogues from taking the village by surprise.

As time marched on, of course, the need for such warnings had diminished, but it hadn't stopped the residents of Copper Falls from adopting the raven as their protector and mascot.

Over the years, the ravens had marked the start of certain events, with a deafening ruckus and a darkening of the skies, as they'd taken flight. Local history had noted these times and the events that happened the day after – the start of both World Wars, for example.

They had also heralded when something bad was to befall Copper Falls itself, like the kidnap and murder of little Janie Stevens or the hostage situation at the bank, which had left five people dead.

All these events had been before the building of Raven Bridge; before the ravens had disappeared from the town.

My grandmother had often warned me that someday we would be sorry for forcing them to leave, but I had just nodded, too young to really understand.

The last documented "raven uproar" had happened the day before completion of Raven Bridge. The aesthetics of the village had changed dramatically and my grandmother, apparently, had complained about it constantly. She had been the last remaining protestor as my grandfather had towered over her in his bulldozer. He had never forgiven her.

This particular day the sun had been beating down and the sky had been the deep clear blue of summer. The constant drone of the bulldozers had been an all too familiar sound in Copper Falls, so much so that when the ravens had kicked off, everyone had stopped to stare; even the contractors.

The whole town had put it down to the birds protesting at the destruction of their habitat. Even the historical society hadn't noted the disturbance at first; not until the following day, when the town had awoken to an uneasy silence; to an absence of ravens.

Around lunchtime, my grandfather had been discovered

crushed under his bulldozer. To this day, no one knows how it had happened.

My grandmother, stoic to the end, had never shed a tear for him.

'He deserved it, Jake,' she'd said to me one day. 'He should never have led the destruction of that wood. If he hadn't, they'd still be here and he'd still be alive.'

I hadn't known what to say so, quiet child that I was, I'd said nothing.

'Mark my words, Jake,' she'd continued. 'Those ravens will be back, but it won't be a warning they'll bring with them.'

My grandmother had passed away in her sleep that night, leaving me alone and at the mercy of the authorities.

She'd been right as well. The ravens did come back. Twenty men had worked on the building of that bridge and every last one of them was dead within a year; all killed within the vicinity of Raven Bridge; all in freak accidents; all watched over by the ravens and by me. It was after this horrific year that the locals renamed it "Death Bridge".

One by one they were picked off. No one saw the pattern, except me. No one really connected the two; or didn't want to. My own theories, especially the ones which said they hadn't finished, were beaten into silence. But I'd been right.

Eventually, I'd been right. It took twenty years, though.

Two decades after the deaths of the men involved in the building of Raven Bridge, their descendants started to be picked off; one by one; Peter Johns being the first. Slowly. Methodically. Calculatingly. Their raucous cry afterwards, reminded me of laughter; harsh, unfeeling laughter; laughter that punctuated the lesson they were teaching.

It's funny really. After all the deaths I'd witnessed over the years, I couldn't imagine what it would feel like when my turn came.

Strangely, I don't feel anything. As I stare up at the beady black eyes of the ravens, lined up along Raven Bridge, I feel calm, almost accepting of my fate; a fate bestowed on me by my grandfather.

I hear the screech of brakes and I hear the voices screaming at me to get out of the road. I turn around to face my fate and smile to see the construction vehicle bearing down. The irony is not lost on me.

I close my eyes and raise my face to the heavens. The last thing I hear is the harsh laughter of the ravens as they leave Raven Bridge for the last time; their numbers swelled by one; their unkindness complete.

THE END

5 SUPERSTITIOUS NONSENSE

It's funny really, the things your parents tell you when you're growing up - don't sit so close to the television, or you'll get square eyes; if the wind changes direction you'll stay like that; it's bad luck to walk under ladders; don't point at a rainbow; salute at a single magpie. The list goes on. Of course, you don't really believe what they tell you, or should I say, you don't, once you've tested the theories. But what about the superstitions that your friends tell you? Well, they might not actually be called superstitions; more like "urban myths" really. Like the escaped lunatic banging a lover's head on the top of the car whilst his fiancée sits terrified inside. What about these? Do you believe these? Do you dare to test these theories?

We did, or should I say, I did. The others had supposedly already done it and now it was my turn. That is, if I wanted to hang out with them, then I had to do it. You've got to understand my motivation. The thing is, there was this girl. Yes, I know, there's always a girl, but I can promise you this story does not have a happy ending.

Jenna was gorgeous. Long dark hair tied back with a velvet ribbon and those amazing eyes. Navy blue. I have never seen eyes like that before; they just drank you in. She was clever, good at sports, had loads of friends and every guy wanted to date her; including me. But did she know I existed. I'll say not. Why you might ask? Picture this - a non-descript fifteen year old with horn rimmed glasses, thick cable knit jumpers, a "pudding bowl" haircut, quiet, teacher's pet and the nickname of "Alien". Don't ask; I have absolutely no idea why they called me that, but they did.

Anyway, I didn't really have any friends. No one wanted to be pals with someone who was liked by the teachers. To top it all, I was also rubbish at sport – all sport. I spent my time on my computer, in cyber space, where no one knew what I looked like.

The school dance was coming up and I really wanted to go, but, of course, didn't have a date. Pete and Andy, the class jocks, decided it might be a good idea to take me under their wing. I don't know why. I suspect it was a bet. I never did find out; it just didn't seem important in the end.

My better judgment was obviously clouded by thoughts of Jenna on my arm and me being the envy of all the other guys. Me, Alien, going to the dance with the goddess. I did have the good sense to ask them what I had to do to earn this help, before I actually committed myself. To be honest, their requests, although very wrong and against everything I believed in as an upstanding and honest human being, didn't seem impossible. Here, see for yourself:

1. Steal money from my dad.

2. Break into one of the teacher's cars and take something.

3. Walk naked through the girls changing rooms - whilst they were in there.

4. Tell Ms Smethers that I loved her - in front of the whole class.

5. Stand before a mirror in a darkened room and say the alphabet backwards.

You have to understand, I would do anything for Jenna. Just the chance to spend time with her. For this, I was willing to become a thief, a flasher and a complete idiot. I just hoped that one day she'd appreciate the effort I'd gone to. I was a little perplexed by the last request, but I thought I'd ask more about it when I'd got the others out of the way.

As you can imagine, I ended up in all sorts of trouble. I got caught stealing twenty pence from my dad's bedside drawer and received the hiding of my life. I swear, I still flinch when I go to sit down and it happened years ago. The car break in didn't go too well either. They didn't warn me that the car was alarmed and monitored by the police. Well, a night in a cell was deemed punishment enough to stop me doing it again and believe me, sharing a cell with a drunk and a raving lunatic did just that. The most humiliating of all though, wasn't being made to stand naked in front of the whole school during assembly for having streaked through the girls' changing room. No, the most humiliating was declaring my undying love for Ms Smethers. She was old and I mean grandparent old. She was fat, had grey hair and had a really hairy mole on her top lip. I think she actually took me seriously because she kept winking at me after that and offering me lifts home; much to my horror.

Pete and Andy, of course, thought this was hilarious. You've got to understand the importance of me being accepted by these two guys and, hence, being in a position to be looked at by Jenna. Pete was the captain of the football team. He was tall and good looking, in a smooth city trader kind of way. He had dark curly hair and hooded eyes which gave him that moody look that girls, for reasons beyond comprehension, always seem to go for. Andy, on the other hand, was blonde and a bit rough around the edges. He had blue eyes, a killer smile and was the star of the basketball team. Yep, he was tall and yep, the girls adored him. So, really, being accepted by these two was a win-win situation for me.

Anyway, the day came for the last assignment. I was feeling pretty good as I'd done all the others, suffered the punishment and humiliation and was mere steps away from the love of my life. I was even getting cocky which, for me, was totally unheard of.

'So, what's with this mirror and alphabet stuff?' I said. We were in my bedroom with the curtains closed and, despite it being the middle of the day, the room was almost pitch dark. That's blackout curtains for you.

'You mean you've never heard of it before?' said Pete.

'Nope,' I said, walking nonchalantly around my room. 'What's the deal?'

'The deal,' Andy said, 'is that you have to stand in front of that mirror and say the alphabet backwards.' He was pointing at the circular mirror above my chest of drawers.

'Doh, I know that much,' I said, 'but what's the deal? What's supposed to happen? I assume something's supposed to happen.'

'Yeah, something's supposed to happen all right,' Pete said, sniggering. 'You've got to promise to do it, even if we tell you what it is, though,' he continued, his face deadly serious.

'What is it?' I was starting to get a bit nervous now.

'You still gonna do it or what?' Andy said.

'Of course,' I said, not sounding convinced, even to me.

'Well, as the superstition goes,' Pete began, 'if you stand

in front of a mirror in a darkened room and say the alphabet backwards, then a werewolf will appear behind you.'

'You're joking, right?' I finally said, the colour having drained from my face. If there was one thing I was scared of, it was horror films, especially those with werewolves. These two knew this - from English - when we'd had to write an essay about our fears and I'd been chosen to read mine out. The jibes and taunts had gone on for months after that. It had been awful. I thought they'd forgotten all about it. Obviously not.

'No, we're not joking. Come on, Alien, we've done it. You're not scared are you?' Andy said and they both started laughing.

'No, I'm not scared,' I muttered. If the truth be told, though, I was terrified.

'Well, come on then. Jenna won't go to the dance with you if you can't even do something as childish as this. You do want to go out with her don't you, Alien?'

'Y…y…yes.'

'Well, get on with it then. It's only a story, Alien. You don't actually believe in werewolves do you?' Pete said, before erupting into raucous laughter.

I could feel the anger and the fear welling up inside me and I stared into the mirror, gripping the edge of the chest of drawers so hard that my knuckles went white. I could see them both in the mirror, laughing, joking and poking fun at me. All the hatred for all the things they'd ever done to me came bubbling to the surface. I swallowed it all back down and took a deep breath. Focusing on my own reflection, I started.

'Z, Y, X, W, V, U, T, S, R, Q, P, O, N, M, L, K, J, I, H, G, F, E, D, C, B, A.'

I closed my eyes and held my breath. Superstition or not, I didn't want to see. My stomach was in knots as it was. I felt physically sick and my skin was starting to itch and my head to ache.

'Bloody hell, Danny, you did it. I honestly thought you were too chicken shit to do it,' said Pete, a certain amount of admiration in his voice.

'Well, did you see anything then?' said Andy, excitement edging his voice.

'No,' I said, my voice unusually deep and hoarse. 'I had my eyes closed. I didn't want to see, just in case.'

'So you are chicken shit,' snorted Pete. 'I knew it! Come on Andy, we're outta here. I'm not spending any more time with this loser.'

'I don't feel too good,' I said and turned around to face them. I felt dreadful. I could feel the sweat dripping off me; my stomach was cramping and my back was aching, forcing me to double over in pain. I looked up at Pete and

Andy, but I could hardly see them. My vision was tinted red. I shook my head to try and clear it, but that just made it worse. It felt like my whole face was stretching. The pain was unbelievable and as I dropped my face into my hands, all I saw were claws.

'Help me!' I shouted at them, but all that came out was a growl.

What was happening to me? I moved towards them and reached out, but they just backed away from me; screaming; terrified. The pain was overwhelming. I felt as though I was going to faint. I was losing control over my limbs, but they were still moving. I could feel the blackness pervade my vision as their screams echoed in my head and then there was nothing.

Pete and Andy stared in horror at the thing in front of them. This wasn't supposed to happen. It was a stupid myth; a story; superstitious nonsense. Everyone knew that those stories weren't true.

Neither of them moved, but whether this was through choice was up for debate. All they could do at first was stare. In amazement? In horror? In fear? Whatever it was, they didn't move for what seemed an eternity. They watched as Danny changed into their worst nightmare.

His body stretched and contorted until he was forced

forwards onto all fours, his hands and feet morphing into the paws of a huge wild dog; his nails elongating and thickening into claws. Coarse hair spread across his body, but it was his face that had them transfixed. His ears were now pointed; his face stretched to form a long snout; his eyes were red as blood - devils eyes; and his teeth were long and sharp. As the creature opened its jaws and growled at them, Andy finally lost control of his bladder. The stench of ammonia filled the air and as the creature started to move towards them, both boys began to scream.

Pete made a break for the bedroom door, but he was too slow. The creature gripped him around the neck and dragged him forward. Pete stared straight into its eyes and felt fear clutch his heart so tightly, he thought it would stop beating. Perhaps that would have been best. The creature snapped his neck and hurled him against the bedroom wall; the plaster crumbling under the impact.

Andy was crying by now; rooted to the spot. He could hear sirens outside and footsteps on the stairs as people came running. He knew, though, that they wouldn't get here in time. The creature stood between him and the door; there was no way out. Andy closed his eyes and dropped to his knees, curling up like a baby. He didn't want to see it anymore; didn't want to know when it was coming for him. He heard the thud of its paws as they carried its weight towards him and he felt the dampness of its nose as it pushed against him, nuzzling him like a pet dog would, before it started licking him. It licked his ears, his neck, his hair and then the rough tongue reached down and licked his cheek. Andy almost smiled, it kind of tickled, but then he remembered. He shuddered as bile flooded into his throat. He didn't see the creature's jaws open, but he did feel its teeth as they locked around his head like a vice and slowly began to tighten.

Seconds later a hollow snap could be heard, then a thud and then nothing.

I felt the pain sear through my head as something was shone into my eyes. I tried to blink, but someone was holding my eyelids open. I tried to brush them out of the way, but my arms were secured by my sides.

'He's coming around.' I heard someone say and then I heard footsteps. The light had disappeared and my vision was clearing; the red tinge having dissipated. Mum and dad came into my line of sight and I tried to smile at them, but I couldn't move. I tried to speak to them, but I couldn't. My mouth wouldn't move. I looked at mum quizzically, but she just turned away, tears streaming down her cheeks.

'I'm sorry, son. They had no choice. Not after what you did,' my dad said.

I had absolutely no idea what he was talking about. I don't know whether he sensed this or just wanted to rub it in, but he told me what the police had found when they'd burst into my bedroom.

Pete's body had been in a heap on the floor, his neck broken and every other bone in his body shattered. He had been hurled with great force against the wall, so hard in fact, that there was now a hole in the bedroom wall. Andy's body had been found curled up in a ball under the window; headless. His head had been torn from his neck and had been found lying next to me; his eyes wide and staring. I had been found unconscious on the floor, shivering and covered in blood, or more to the point, my face had been covered in blood. In fact, my mouth had been full of blood and traces of hair; Andy's hair.

'This is why you have been restrained, why you have a clamp over your mouth. You did that to those boys. You!' He shook his head in shame.

I just stared at my dad. *They honestly believed that I had done that?* I couldn't move; I couldn't speak; and I couldn't explain what had gone on in that room. I couldn't explain to them how sick I'd felt; how my body had felt like it had been taken over by something. I couldn't tell them I had blacked out. I started shaking my restraints. I needed to explain. *Christ, I hadn't done this! I was half their size. How can anyone believe that I would be capable of something like this?*

'Calm down, Danny.' I heard my dad say, but I wasn't listening. I needed to get out of these restraints; I needed to get this thing off my mouth; I needed to explain. I could feel the anger and resentment rising through my body. I could feel my blood pulsing in my temples and as I stared at my dad, imploring him to do something, the red mist started to cloud my vision.

I could feel the sickness in my stomach again and the sweat breaking out all over my body. I shook myself as hard as I could to try to break the restraints. My jaw muscles were working overtime to try to work the clamp loose. I squeezed my eyes shut and took a deep breath and with all the strength I had, I pulled against the restraints. I heard my mum scream and an alarm sounded above my bed. I could hear footsteps in the corridor as security ran to my room. They wouldn't get here in time.

The sound of snapping leather and exploding metal filled the hospital room and the corridors soon resonated with the guttural howl of the werewolf.

THE END

6 SHEER HELL

I have two friends. We've been together since childhood. We do everything together. We're inseparable. We have a bond; a special bond. That's why we were here; at Clogwyn Goch and the gaping crack of "Hellsmouth".

'C'mon, Ed. You've always wanted to climb it,' Flash's voice echoed.

'Yeah, we've climbed higher than this in our sleep,' Muggy's voice chipped in.

'But this one's never been successfully climbed before,' I muttered. My head was pounding and their images kept flashing, like synapses snapping in my brain. I shook my head to try to clear it and reached in my pocket for my tablets. I pulled out the empty bottle and stared at it. I should have got it refilled days ago.

I stood at the base of the wall and looked up the face. It leant out over me, darkening the shadow in which I stood.

There was a story that the place itself was cursed; haunted by the souls of witches, burned at the stake at its summit and then hurled into the river at its base. Now dammed, the dry riverbed remained as a barren ribbon below. Local historians had excavated the area, but had never found any human remains. Inquests into the climbing fatalities had always ruled them as "deaths by misadventure"; due to lapses in concentration, gear failure, poor placement and the like.

The first pitches passed without any real difficulty and I soon got into my rhythm; scaling the face with easy, fluid movement. I could hear their voices echoing off the wall as they taunted each other about this easy move or that tough pull. I preferred to climb in silence. They knew this.

The rock face was almost red from a distance, but close up it was kind of mottled. It had a smooth surface with small pink crystals glistening, despite the shade. In places, red threads ran through it, almost like veins. I ran my finger along one of the thicker veins and the image of a rock fall flashed into my mind. I jerked my hand away from the wall and lost my footing, muttering expletives as I bounced on the end of the rope.

'Careful!' Flash's voice sounded.

'Climbing again,' I shouted back, as I managed to regain the face. I clung to the wall to calm myself and listened as the rocks I'd dislodged clattered away into the riverbed, now far below.

'Come on, you clumsy git,' Muggy's voice echoed across the face. 'We've got this licked, easy.'

I looked up at the route and caught glimpses of them, a good fifty or sixty feet above me, almost halfway up the wall. That's when I heard it; a low rumble; almost like an earthquake. Then I felt what seemed like a ripple through the rock face. Then I saw it. At first, I thought it was just birds passing in front of the sun, but as I shielded my eyes from the glare, the shapes tumbled silently through space, getting bigger and bigger as they fell.

'Look out,' I screamed, but it was too late. Through the glare, I saw the rocks crash against his helmet. His body crumpled and he fell backwards off the wall, his impatience in belaying now costing dear. The cam came clean out of the rock face, as if the rock had just let go.

'Muggy!' I screamed, frozen to the wall, watching, as he bounced against it again and again; the pull of the rope dragging him in, before leaving him pirouetting limp at its end.

Panic set in as I frantically locked off the rope, clipping into better placements. I closed my eyes and saw Muggy's body spinning lazily in space. Tears welled as my heart thundered in my chest. I called his name, again and again, but it was no use. Another image flashed through my mind; a rope; a frayed rope.

'Flash,' I shouted. 'We need to get down, right now.' I heard him swear as I was about to start my descent.

'What's up?' I yelled.

'Rope's stuck on something.'

I looked up and could just about make out the image of him yanking at the rope above him. I saw the picture of the frayed rope again and then I felt the ripple through the rock, followed by the deep rumbling. Above the pendulum of Muggy's body, Flash's rope rubbed against the small shiny crystals of rock.

'Don't move. Get some gear in now and hang on tight,' I called. He carried on yanking at the rope.

I yelled again, just as he gave one final pull and the rope snapped. I heard his screams as he lost his balance and fell away from the wall. I watched in horror as the gear at the top gave out and their bodies tumbled through the air in slowly rotating spirals. I closed my eyes and felt the rush of air as they hurtled passed me to land, with a sickening thud, in the riverbed.

'I'm okay. I'm okay,' I muttered and looked across at the cam, in the crack next to me, which held my weight. It was slowly walking out of the rock. What the hell was going on?

'Secure yourself now. This one's going to give, any minute,' I shouted; my mind spinning; my sanity vanishing. I started to edge sideways. I was only a few feet away and if I could just get to it, I would be able to secure it again. I grabbed a nut and reached as far as I could. Just as I was about to jam it in, the wall seemed to literally "spit" it out again.

I looked down at the twisted bodies in the riverbed below. Another ripple went through the wall and I looked at the cam and saw it was almost free. Frantic to belay, I stabbed at the crack with different nuts, but nothing was holding. This could not be happening. How could this rock reject the gear?

'Noooooo!' I shouted and smashed gear repeatedly into the rock face. I heard the rumble before I felt it this time. The image that appeared in my mind was fuzzy, hard to make out, as though it hadn't been decided yet.

I didn't waste any more time. I had to get down; fast. I could hear the rocks falling from the top of the wall and I kept myself as close as I could to the rock face. Some struck me, with sharp stinging pain, before splintering on the riverbed below. I hardly noticed. I placed six nuts as quickly as I could, the rock seeming to resist my attempts. All I could do was scramble down using the rope. I just hoped I would have enough time before the wall spewed out the nuts, which I knew it would.

My arms screaming in protest, I started to descend, desperately grasping rock and rope, abandoning safety for speed. I had to get off the face.

I felt the ripple run up the wall again and then I felt myself drop as the nuts were forced out of the wall, one by one. I just focused on the riverbed. Eighty feet to go. That was all I had and then I'd be safe.

I felt the rope go slack. There was nothing left to hold me to the wall. Handholds seemed to melt away and footholds dissolved beneath my rock shoes. I allowed my body to go limp as I fell, the air whistling passed me. The rope jarred as each of the remaining nuts were expelled from the rock. As the last protection was vomited out of the wall, I could swear I heard a deep guttural laugh.

The impact was harder and faster than I could've imagined. The pain instantaneous. Femurs snapped. Bones ruptured the skin. I looked down to see blood seeping through my trouser legs. Then a numbing blackness and laughter; maddeningly absurd laughter; the laughter of euphoria; the laughter of a lunatic. As I blacked out, I realised it was mine.

For all my dreams of conquering the route, I got my glory. My name finally appeared in "Climb Magazine", just not in the manner I had anticipated:

"Celebrated climber, John "Ed" Edwards, was found

today at the bottom of Clogwyn Goch, following a solo climb, suffering from severe hypothermia and blood loss, due to multiple compound fractures. Edwards, a functional schizophrenic, had even set up a camera to film his ascent and police are now examining the footage. He believed that, after a life of climbing the living rock, it had finally rejected him. Once his condition has stabilised, Edwards will be moved to a secure mental facility."

I do miss Muggy and Flash, but they've put me back on my tablets now, so the chances of new friends appearing are non-existent.

THE END

7 IN MEMORY OF

'Stay on the path. Whatever you do, don't go on the moors.' It's a line I'd heard so often whilst growing up. A line immortalised in *An American Werewolf in London*. A line I'd got so sick of hearing as a child, that I never thought I'd forget it. But I did.

Of course, we were never told why we couldn't go on the moors. We were kids; we were too young to know the reasons why. They didn't have to tell us though; our rampant imaginations were enough to keep us away. But when we reached puberty, everything that the adults said was bullshit. It was as if we lived on different planets and spoke a different language. We never thought we needed to remember anything they said. Well, until that night anyway.

I shudder as I remember that night. People said I'd been lucky. They couldn't understand how I'd survived; they had said God himself must have been protecting me. *What the hell did they know?* I've had to live with it; I've had to live with the aftermath every day since. Every day for fifteen years.

I stand here now, staring out at the moors; at the barren wasteland, haunted by so many memories. It's kind of comforting for me coming back here every year. I feel at peace here; where it happened. Of course, no one wants to know me. They say I'm cursed. They say I bring death on the village whenever I come back. But I still come. I have to. It's all part of the cycle.

Of course, their hatred of me isn't new. It started about a month after the attacks. I was still in hospital. I became delirious one night, so the nurses said, and I became violent. They said my eyes changed. They said it was like looking into hell itself. They said I became uncontrollable, so much so, that they had to restrain me; had to sedate me. I don't remember. After that, things changed.

It's getting dark; the fog settling over the moors; the wind rippling through my hair. It won't be long now. Soon they will come and it will happen again, just like it did then. I remember back to that night and I shudder. How was I to know how it would change me.

My dad had called us the *Witches of Eastwick*. I was the quiet blonde, Ali was the sultry brunette and Ginnie was the seductive red head. We had been inseparable and we were always giggling and whispering; hence our nickname. We did everything together and we were known around the village as "the witches". Wherever one of us was; then so were the other two.

Our village was a bit strange. It was split into two by a half-mile strip of moorland, which then mushroomed out into dense moors. That night we, the witches, had been invited to Janie's fifteenth birthday sleepover. She'd lived over the other side and we'd set off about seven thirty. It had been a cold, damp November night. We'd all had our goodies – our make-up, music, booze and cigarettes. Ali had even managed to steal some weed from her brother. It had been going to be one hell of a party.

'Don't stray off the path,' my mother had called.

'Whatever,' I'd replied and we'd set off giggling, teasing and giving marks out of ten to the new hunk at school.

I can't remember how far across we were, when I'd first heard it – an unearthly howl resonating across the moors - but it had stopped me in my tracks.

'What was that?' I'd whispered.

'What was what?' Ginnie had said, giggling as she'd dragged on a joint, before she'd passed it on to Ali. But then the howl had echoed again in the still night, closer this time; much closer.

'What the hell?' Ali had said.

'Let's just walk,' I'd said and had started to drag her towards the street lamp, glimmering in the distance.

'It's only a dog,' Ginnie had said, running to catch us up. 'What's the problem? We're nearly there.'

Then we'd heard it again and, instinctively, we'd drawn together, backs to each other, hands clasped tightly. I'd felt them both shaking. Ginnie's manicured nails had dug deep into my palm.

'Can you see anything?' Ali had whispered, her usual confident air gone.

'Nothing,' I'd whispered back. 'Can you Ginnie?'

'No, but what's that smell?'

I'd inhaled deeply and had regretted it straight away. Smell had been too mild a word; stench had been closer. The stench of wet dog and rotting flesh. I'd felt bile rise in my throat and had fought to keep it down.

'Can you breathe a bit more quietly you two; it'll hear us!' Ali had hissed.

'It's not me,' we'd both said and I'd felt us all tense up, as the same thought must have passed through our minds. The breathing had been slow and laboured, as if it had been running.

'I still can't see anything,' I'd whispered.

'Me neither,' replied Ali, but Ginnie had been silent. I had felt her shaking as she clung to my hand and the smell of ammonia had been sharp in my nostrils. My body had filled with dread and I'd been turning to look when my arm had been almost yanked out of my socket.

'Arghhh!' Ginnie had screamed.

'Ginnie!' I'd yelled, as Ali and I had whirled around, but it had been too late. The animal had been tearing into her already lifeless body. Her head had been lolling to one side; her beautiful emerald eyes dead and staring. Her neck had been ripped open, exposing flesh and bone and it had started to tear the rest of her apart, snuffling and growling as it had done so.

'Noooooo!' I'd screamed and had lunged at the animal, but it had been too quick for me. Pain had seared through my side as I'd been flung to the ground and I'd felt the warmth of blood soaking through my clothes.

'Megan!' Ali had shouted and had started running towards me.

'Run Ali! Run!' I'd shouted, but it had been too late. It had pounced as she'd turned. I'd heard her clothes and her flesh ripping apart as it had brought her down. I'd closed my eyes, unable to move, as it had started to tear into her body. Its jaws burrowing deep into her gut, dragging her insides out.

The gunshot had made me jump and the animal had yelped, before it had hit the ground with a thud. I opened my eyes to see Janie's dad running towards us and then I'd blacked out.

I shudder as I remember my parents talking about the state of my friends. The caskets had been closed for obvious reasons. I wish I could've been there, but they wouldn't let me out of the hospital. They said it was for my own safety.

I remember visiting their graves a few weeks after leaving hospital and being shocked at what I'd seen. In contrast to the rest of the grassed cemetery, Ali and Ginnie's graves were stone caskets. But it wasn't that which I found shocking; it was the inscriptions on the side. It looked like some kind of spell and it was etched in silver. Of course, I know what the writing is now. It's a containment spell; a spell to keep the evil in, not out. It took me five years to find that out and I had to go through many people to do so. But at least then I knew. I knew what had happened that night and I knew what the rest of my life would be like.

For a while after the attacks, things had been okay and I'd truly believed that life would return to normal. People had been nice to me, but had refused to talk about what had happened. Then one day it had changed. That was the night I had become delirious and violent. Ever since then, doors had been closed to me. Not a soul had crossed my path and even my parents had made themselves scarce. Eventually, I'd moved away; to start afresh where no one knew me and more importantly, where no one knew what had happened to me.

I have a new life now, a husband, a daughter and a great career; but I have to go away from them every few weeks. I don't want them to see the demons that lurk inside me.

I pad through the village now, on this crisp night. Nothing has changed. The streets are deserted; the doors and windows firmly closed. No one is welcome. I laugh to myself, a deep guttural laugh; almost a growl. God help any visitors who should come. Lucky for me, though, there are always visitors.

I wander back to the moors; to that place. I stretch to loosen myself up and sit down to wait. I turn and stare up at the moon, ripe and full, and a guttural howl erupts from inside me; resonating across the deserted moors.

THE END

8 HOW DOES YOUR GARDEN GROW?

'Why do I do it? Honestly, it all started with a thought I had one day – the thought that I could just randomly kill someone and I wouldn't feel a thing – and I haven't. Not a flicker. It's almost like I'm dead inside, but I'm not. What it does do, even if only temporarily, is release the tight fist of anger and hate that resides in my chest. The freedom I feel is like a drug. I feel euphoric; I feel free and I feel alive. The bottom line is, I feel.

So, let me take you on a journey into my world; the world of a serial killer. It takes three kills to achieve that status and I've way surpassed that. So, grab your coat and let's go hunting.'

I stared at the man before me; so beautiful; so confident. So, why did he do what he did? Why did he treat them like they didn't matter? Like they were toys that could be picked up and dropped again on a whim? They weren't toys; they were people. They felt, they loved and they hurt, and he needed to understand exactly what pain was. Maybe then, he'd realise the impact of his actions.

'Please, please let me go,' he said, tears seeping from the corners of his eyes.

The plastic crackled under my feet as I stepped forward. I couldn't take my eyes off him. He was gorgeous, sculpted from marble like Michelangelo's David; his body was divine. His hair, dark and tousled an hour ago, lay matted with sweat against his skull. His piercing blue eyes; eyes that had made my heart skip a beat; now showed only fear.

I stuffed a rag soaked in cloves into his mouth. I needed silence from him for my work and I loved the smell of cloves.

He was spread-eagled on what he'd believed to be my bed. Men are all the same. I haven't met one who would turn down the chance of no questions asked sex. The shock on his face when I'd shoved him down onto his current resting place - a marble slab - had made me smile. His head had slammed against the marble, stunning him long enough for me to snap the handcuffs shut and turn up the lights. The seductive boudoir he'd imagined had been transformed into the torture chamber it really was.

When I pressed play on my iPod, the harsh notes of Berlioz' *Symphonie Fantastique* flooded the room. I closed my eyes and tuned in, letting the music wash through me, connecting with the black ball at my core. I snapped on latex gloves and turned to face my blank canvas; the tools of my trade laid out neatly, waiting for me to make my choice.

Scalpel first, I thought. The music suffusing my body, caused my hand to almost dance. With the tip pressed against his smooth, flawless cheek, I applied just enough pressure to break the skin. Usually, I would wait for the music to move my hand and create my masterpiece, but my latest canvas decided he wanted to do it himself. I held my hand still, watching the picture emerge, as he tossed his head from side to side in a desperate attempt to avoid the blade. If only he'd used his brain. Too pretty; too cocksure; too vain. A bubble of pleasure bounced off the blackness inside me and I caught a sliver of light.

I traced the scalpel down over his chin, leaving a path from the mosaic of his face, hovering over his carotid artery until his whimpering and shuddering almost brought my pleasure to an end. The journey continued to his chest; his pumped, waxed and tanned pectoral muscles. My scalpel sank cleanly into each muscle and I watched the blood surface and fan out like poppies across the canvas. Poppies had centres, didn't they – dark ones? I cut deeper into the muscle, carving a circular centre in each pectoral; my pliers serving to pull the flesh back, creating a perfect centre for my poppies.

My canvas, however, was doing his best to ruin everything, by tensing whenever I touched him. This caused the blood to pump more, threatening to spoil my design. What to do?

My tray of tools glistened in the overhead light. *Which one would do the job?* My gaze settled on the heaviest object – the wrench. I picked it up and ran my fingers along its length before brushing its cold hard surface against my cheek. I shuddered. Then, raising my arm above my head, I brought it down hard on his temple. Bone crunched and then his body went limp. Good; now I could work.

My favourite flowers of all are daisies; the multitude of petals reflecting the multiple facets of my personality. Daisies, however, do not have dark centres, but you have to work with what you've got, when you're an artist.

I flicked each of his nipples to see if I got a response and gently massaged them until they became hard - men! I selected my next implement - the nail clippers – and knowing the firmness wouldn't last long, I clipped each nipple off and placed them in a plastic tub for later use; maybe. The ruby liquid bubbled to the surface and I shivered with pleasure. Then, I realised my mistake. My canvas started to flood. Dammit!

Luckily, I always kept additional supplies for just such

emergencies. I grabbed the salt and poured it into the two wounds, rubbing it in firmly to try to soak up enough of the blood to allow me to finish. I brushed the excess away and pressed the remainder into the wounds before leaning in close to carve the delicate daisy petals around each aureole.

The use of the salt was starting to bring my canvas around. Never mind; I'd want him awake soon anyway.

A paintbrush served to disband any leftover salt and I concentrated on joining my poppies and daisies together with interconnecting stems, which finished at his navel. Finished with my scalpel for the time being, I picked up a piece of bamboo cane and some garden twine. It was time to create the centrepiece.

It always amazed me how small the penis could make itself when under threat. It certainly wasn't this small when he first got here. He had been ever so proud of it. Let's see what he thinks when I've finished with it.

He needed to be awake for this. He needed to feel the pain that I was about to inflict on his most prized organ; the same organ he'd used to bring so much pain to others. I grabbed the bucket of water at my feet, emptied it over his head and took the rag out of his mouth.

'You fucking bitch! What the…' I tuned out. I'd heard it all before.

I picked the cane up and took a length of twine,

securing the cane to the base of his penis. I then pulled the penis as tall as it would go and wrapped two more pieces of twine around it. Didn't want it collapsing before I was finished now, did I?

The obscenities kept coming, but that would change very soon. Next, I picked up a pair of very sharp nail scissors and went to work on the creation of my centrepiece. *Oh yes, the obscenities soon changed, didn't they?* I smiled. To say he sounded like a wounded animal was an understatement.

Once I'd finished, I peeled the petals down, revealing the plump, vulnerable core of my lotus flower.

Next, I picked up a length of stiffened wire with a brightly coloured butterfly on the end; the picture I was creating, clear in my mind.

'No, no, please, no more. I'm sorry. Whatever it is I've done to you, I'm sorry,' my canvas pleaded.

My hand hovered just above the centre of the flower. 'This isn't about me. This is about the rest of them,' I said as I began to push the wire deep into his core.

A thrill bubbled through me as I watched his body contort as he tried to curl in on himself in self-preservation. His howls could be heard for miles around, if there was anyone to hear them, but there wasn't.

I stopped pushing as the butterfly hovered just above

the centre of the lotus flower, ready to alight. Pleased with the effect, I pondered my next tool of choice – scissors or carving knife? It was going to be scissors, as it was a very slow and painful way to do what I was going to do, but I opted for the carving knife. I hadn't used it in a while and I liked to have a change every now and then.

The knife glinted in the light and I held it up so he could see it. I now needed to relocate my centrepiece. He was watching me; I could see him out of the corner of my eye. I don't suppose this had happened very often to him - a woman having him by the balls. I brought the knife to the core of his being; to the centre of his world. I smiled when I saw his expression change as the penny dropped or, should I say, thudded.

'N…n…no please. I'll undo it. Whatever it is, I'll make it right. Don't cut my cock off, I beg you.'

'There is nothing you can do,' I said, jabbing the tip of the knife under his chin. 'You've already done enough; ruined too many lives; conned too many women into believing you're a good guy. You make me sick!'

With that I started to carve. At first, he screamed, but as with all of them, the pain soon overcame him and he passed out. Once again, Berlioz and I were alone. I hummed along to the music as I sliced through muscle, tendons and ligaments until my lotus flower was finally free. Not wishing to disturb my work, I gently removed the splint and placed the flower on his navel; at the base of the intertwining stems.

Finally, I released his hands from the cuffs and arranged them so they cupped the lotus flower. Of course, they wouldn't stay in place of their own accord, but I found a nine inch nail hammered through the back of each hand into those carefully sculpted abdominal muscles, did the trick.

As my final act, I slashed his carotid and femoral arteries with the scalpel and watched as the blood pumped from his body into the receptacles below. He never regained consciousness, which was a shame.

I picked up a paintbrush and artists' canvas and, dipping the brush in his blood, I proceeded to write:

TO ALL MY VICTIMS; I AM TRULY SORRY.

I then placed the canvas between his legs and, going to my camera mounted tripod, I viewed my masterpiece, before capturing the image for my collection.

I'm sure he was sorry. They usually are, by the time I've finished with them.

I took a deep breath and exhaled. The blackness was gone again, for now.

'So, this is what I do. I don't believe I am doing anything

wrong. I believe I am bringing justice to all the women these men have wronged. Why? Because our judicial system consistently fails to do so.

I am lucky, though. I live in the middle of nowhere so no one can see or hear anything. To my knowledge, no one has seen me with these men, but I am aware that this may not be the case. So, really, the only person who knows is you and I am telling you because I want the real story to come out when I'm caught, which I know I will be - one day. I want these women to know that someone was fighting for them.

I suppose you want to know how I get rid of the bodies. Well, that's a story for another time. Goodbye.'

I disconnected the call and leant back in my sun longer, surveying the beauty of my garden. It is truly stunning. The colours; the variety; the longevity. If people were to ask, I would tell them that it's all in the fertiliser.

THE END

9 THE LAST DANCE

I stood there waiting for him to leave, but of course, he couldn't. He was trapped and I was the one who had trapped him. I had to laugh, though. It was my own stupidity; my own cockiness that had got me into this situation and now look at me. I was more than a little uneasy. I mean, I'd never been trapped anywhere with him before. There had always been a way out; for both of us. But not now. Not daring to breathe, I edged to the corner and peered around. Nothing. Shit. Where the hell was he? I pulled back into the relative safety of my corner and closed my eyes.

'Looking for me, by any chance?' My heart almost stopped at the sound of his voice.

'Haven't planned this very well, have you, Jakey boy? Us? Together? It always ends badly for one of us.'

I opened my eyes and looked at him. He was getting old now; I could see it in the deep lines on his face. He was right though, we'd had our tussles over the years, but no one had ever really won. I can't even remember how long ago it was when we had first met, but suffice to say, he had been a lot younger and a lot stronger. So had I. Well, a lot younger at least.

'They were good times, weren't they?' he said, chuckling to himself. I closed my eyes and thought back to the last time I had seen him.

It had been the usual story. Lucas had slipped his tag and had made it to the nearest village before we had even been aware of his absence. He'd put the tag on another inmate, so that a pulse was detected and the alarms hadn't sounded. The deception had been spotted by a guard when the inmates had been fed. This particular inmate had a tag around each wrist. Needless to say, he'd been punished severely for his part in the deception. He hadn't required a tag after that.

By the time I'd got to the village, the dead and wounded had numbered more than ten and I'd had to call for reinforcements. The clean up would take a while. The wounded had to be restrained; the dead had to be incinerated; and the living had to have their memories altered. I had to track down Lucas. I knew him; I knew his tastes; and, more importantly, I knew his MO. There had been a dilapidated barn on the outskirts of the village and, on reaching it, I'd stepped up to the half open door and peered inside. Sure enough, there he'd been, taking advantage of some poor girl. He'd knocked her about a bit beforehand, as had been his way. I had seen the blood dripping from her face. I'd shaken my head in disgust as I'd watched him hunched over her.

'Hello, Lucas,' I'd said. I'd had to give it to him, he'd certainly kept calm; despite having known what would happen to him when he got back. He'd been on his final warning.

'Well, well, well,' he'd said, his body straightening up as he'd turned towards me. 'You took your time, didn't you?' A low guttural laugh had escaped his throat, producing a sneer across his once handsome face.

'Move away from the girl,' I'd said, raising my rifle and aiming at him. He'd done as I'd asked and I'd fired. The dart had struck the girl in the chest, but she hadn't flinched. He'd made sure of that.

'I've got two more down at Fletcher's Barn,' I'd said into my radio.

'Roger that, Serg,' the reply had come back.

My eyes had never left Lucas as I'd reloaded the rifle.

'Time's up, Lucas,' I'd said. 'You've had your chances. You just wouldn't wait for the serum, would you?'

'Can't help what's in your blood, Jakey boy,' he'd said

and had grinned; that blood chilling grin of his.

'Hope you're going to come quietly, Lucas,' I'd said and had aimed the rifle at him.

'Whatever you say, Jakey boy.' He'd raised his hands in the air and his eyes had met mine. I'd seen the hatred there.

I had been so tempted to just kill him; to hell with the consequences, but my conscience hadn't let me. Bloody do-gooders and their "living being" rights. I'd stared right back at him, knowing that it would be the last time that I'd see him alive. Thank God the do-gooders couldn't reach inside the facility. We had our own rules there.

I'd pulled the trigger then, but there had just been a click. Lucas hadn't missed a beat. He'd launched himself for freedom. The trouble was, I'd been in his way. I hadn't moved quickly enough and he'd wounded me. I'd been too shocked to go after him. My head had been spinning at all that the wound had implied. I'd been infected.

That had been ten years ago and much had happened since then. I touched the scar on my cheek and remembered the feeling of emptiness in the pit of my stomach, when I'd realised I would be infected.

'Hostel has escaped,' I'd said, flatly, into my radio and I'd sunk to my knees on the floor of the barn. The voices and footsteps had been a blur and when someone had pointed a gun at me and had asked how I'd got the wound, I'd heard myself say, 'punched, that's all. Get after him.'

The paramedics had stitched me up and when I'd looked at it in the mirror, I'd convinced myself it had been too superficial for infection and that I'd be fine. I'd even started to believe it as, for several months, I'd had no symptoms. Then they'd started. Very slightly. Mood swings; aggression; restlessness. It had only been when I'd been able to hear the conversations of people on the other side of the street and smell meat at eight hundred yards that the reality had hit.

I'd panicked. If anyone had found out, I would have been locked up and destroyed like most of the others. I hadn't wanted that. I had a job to do and I'd been damn well going to do it. There'd been no way I'd become the very thing I'd spent the best part of my life destroying. That's when I'd decided that my only option had been to steal the serum. If I'd told anyone what had happened to me that would have been it. I'd had no choice, had I?

I'd carried on then, as before, and no one had been any the wiser. My unit had tracked Lucas' movements over the years, through the path of destruction he'd left in his wake. For some reason though, we'd never been able to catch him. It had been almost as if he'd known we were coming and so had always been one step ahead of us. It had been as though he'd sensed our approach; like animals sense an attacker.

We'd tracked him here and I'd left word with as many informants as I could that I wanted to meet with him; that we had a score to settle, once and for all. I just hadn't planned for it to go down this way.

The thing was, Lucas didn't know about me. I hadn't seen him in ten years and I'd done my best to keep my infection under wraps. As far as I knew, no one else knew about me. They'd never tracked the theft of the serum to me and it had eventually been forgotten. The problem was, I was having to take more and more serum to keep me sane. The infection raging inside me was getting stronger and harder to control. I didn't know how much longer I could carry on and I'd be damned if I was letting it take over me; I'd be damned if I was going to end up like the rest of them.

That's why I was here. I had to finish Lucas off before I dealt with my problem. I'd never rest until I knew I had got my own back on him. Once he was out of the way, I could take care of myself. I no longer cared about the rules. Lucas had to be stopped and I would do it. After all, I didn't plan on being around to face the consequences.

I cursed again for getting myself locked in here. I had to take my serum at regular intervals. The next one was due in ten minutes. I'd left it in the car. After all, I'd planned a better entrance. I'd never missed taking my serum before. The infection was strong enough as it was, that I constantly lived in fear of it taking over my mind. I didn't have any weapons either. Nothing, except a small solid silver dagger, which I kept as a talisman more than anything else.

'It has to end tonight, Jakey boy. I'm too old and too long in the tooth for this anymore. One way or another, one of us isn't leaving this warehouse tonight.'

I glanced at my watch. Not long now. Soon the battle would commence. I should have ended this a long time ago. I knew he would always haunt me, but he was right. It was time to end it.

I looked out of the window and saw them. Ha, I knew it! Not brave enough to do it on his own. They were crouched in the shadows, not far from us. I could see them though. I could smell them. I snorted with laughter.

'Not up to the job any more, Lucas? Too old and grey now?' I said and started walking towards him, full of bravado for the moment. I saw fear flit across his eyes and then it was gone. He pushed his shoulders back and started towards me.

'Can't do without your backup, can you?' I taunted.

'You never know who else may turn up to interrupt us,' he said. We circled each other, like predators waiting to attack a kill, except we were the kill.

'It won't be long now. Soon the sun will have gone down,' he said.

'What difference does that make? Let's do it now,' I said, my bravado still with me.

'You know I can't do that. It wouldn't be right, really, would it? It's always best to wait for the darkness. There are fewer complications.'

'Fine, if that's the way you want it. It's your funeral,' I said and turned away from him. I went back to my corner and sat down. Soon the situation would be out of my control and, one way or another, it would be over. I looked over at him again and saw he was inching towards the door.

'I don't know where you think you're going, but you can't open that from the inside. No one comes in and no one leaves until we are finished. This is between you and me.'

He faltered slightly, but I'll give him his due, he didn't back down. I don't know who was more scared, him or me. I know we all act like we are brave and everything, but at the end of the day, we are all afraid of dying.

I looked at my watch again. It wouldn't be long now.

Glancing out of the window, I could see the vultures circling. It's a shame I hadn't let the squad know what I was doing. It would have been good to watch another fight, while I waited for my own.

I sat and watched as the shadows became longer and the time drew on. Neither of us spoke to the other. There was nothing to say really. A fight was about to commence. A fight to the death. But who was going to win? The vigilante or the werewolf? One fighting for his life, the other fighting for what he thinks is right. Who is right and who is wrong? I ran my fingers over my scar again. This fight was a long time coming.

I heard scratching and snuffling outside and realised the time was here. The last rays of the day filtered in through the mottled glass and I looked over to the shadowed corner where Lucas was holed up. All I could see were his feet and I stared at them intently, waiting for it to start. His boots were off and soon his feet started to move. Not as in he was moving them, but as in changing shape. I shifted my position to try to get a better look, but the darkening evening took the image away from me. All I could do was listen and wait.

I heard the familiar moans as his body changed and morphed into the monster he had been for so long. I waited patiently, willing my own body to stay calm. I could hear his heavy breathing and the snuffling sounds he was making, probably to try to locate me. He was seeking the scent of a man, which I no longer was.

I could feel the first twitching in my body now, the first signs of what was to come. Although I had witnessed this a thousand times with the inmates in the facility, I had never actually gone through it myself. I suppose it had only been a matter of time, anyway. A matter of time until the serum no longer suppressed the infection. I stood, as I'd been told it was less painful this way, and braced myself. I soon forgot about Lucas, as pain surged through my body and my spine began to arch, throwing me forward onto all fours. I cried out and tears swam in my eyes as I watched my hands elongate into paws and my fingers curl up like a hag's. My fingernails grew into razor sharp claws and thick coarse fur erupted from my pores to swathe my body. A wave of nausea overtook me as my nose and mouth were dragged outwards from the rest of my face. I vomited.

Fully formed, I turned my nose towards the moon and made my first call. My ears soon became attuned to my surroundings and I could hear Lucas' gravelly breathing on the other side of the room.

'Well, old man?' I said; my voice hoarse; my throat dry. I padded towards him, my vision clear now. He still sat in the corner, his back to the wall, his pelt now grey instead of the inky black it used to be.

'So,' he said, standing up and facing me. 'You've finally seen the light, have you?' Then he started to laugh – a deep, throaty howl. From outside, a symphony greeted him and hammering started against the door. Thud! Thud! Thud! It wouldn't take them long.

Before I could reply, Lucas launched himself at me, catching me off guard. His teeth embedded themselves in my throat and started to pull. I could hardly breathe; his jaws were slowly cutting off my air supply. I rolled onto my back, dragging him with me. I positioned my back feet against his stomach and ripped my claws through his belly. He howled in pain and let go of me. I ran for the other side of the room to catch my breath, but he was on me again. His teeth tore into my shoulder, as he landed on my back, and his rear claws ripped through the skin on my hindquarters. I could smell the coppery scent and could feel the blood oozing from the wounds. I threw myself over onto my side and managed to disengage him. The adrenalin was pumping now and I didn't give him the chance to get back on his feet. I spun around and went in for the kill. My teeth punctured his neck and I tossed and turned my head with all the strength I could muster until I heard the flesh tear and I fell backwards. I spat out the matted pelt and went straight back in. He was not recovering from this. This was the end for him. I ripped through his belly, his guts emptying onto the concrete floor. I ripped each and every one of his organs apart with my teeth, his breath becoming shallower and shallower until finally there was nothing, but I didn't stop. Every last bit of him was to be destroyed. I tore limbs from their sockets and as my jaws clenched around his head, the door to the warehouse finally burst open and ten bodies filled the space.

They stared at the scene for a while and then one of them padded forward.

'Leave it, Jake,' he said and I turned to look at him, recognising his red pelt immediately. Doyle. Even more notorious than Lucas, in some ways, and a long time on the run.

'C'mon, Jake. We need to leave,' he said and I relaxed. Lucas' head lolled to one side, his lily-white skin punctured by my teeth. His torso lay agape, devoid of its contents. His limbs lay scattered like firewood. I sat and stared, the feeling of euphoria at my conquest making me howl into the night.

'C'mon. Your lot will be here soon,' Doyle said and beckoned for me to follow him. I watched as they exited the warehouse, becoming men once more before they hit the night air.

I stretched and relaxed, closing my eyes. I felt my body respond, my spine straightening once more. I stood up and followed my clan. I paused at the door and looked back at the blood bath I had made. I smiled. The power; the control; the strength. What a great feeling. How had I shunned this? How had I not wanted this? Until now.

THE END

10 EMBERS

I shivered as I stood in the middle of such devastation. The stone walls, blackened by the fire, remained steadfastly in place, their pride preventing them from giving way to the horror that had engulfed them.

The charred embers crunched beneath my feet as I picked my way through the remains of what had once been my home; our home. The acrid stench of fire and death still permeated the air and as the early morning breeze rippled across my skin, I closed my eyes, remembering that night.

The banqueting hall had looked wonderful and I had shaken my head in amazement at how Marco had managed to do all this without my knowledge. Candles had burned from every conceivable nook and cranny, casting the room in a romantic glow. The heady scent of lilies had clung to me as I'd swept through the room; the arrangements majestic on their pedestals. Two hundred guests had been there that night for the "party of the year", according to the society pages.

'Juliet, my dear, you look stunning and the ceremony was beautiful. I didn't realise Marco was so romantic,' Lady Ashford had said as she'd grasped my gloved hands in her own.

'Thank you, Margot, you're too kind,' I'd replied. 'Marco has definitely outdone himself this time.' I had smiled at the older woman and had nodded politely before moving on.

Opening the door to the kitchens, the succulent aroma of roasting pork had invaded my nostrils. The spit had twisted noiselessly over the open fire as the skin of the swine had hissed and crackled.

'Mrs Brown, how is everything going in here?' I'd said. 'Do you need any more help?'

'No, Ma'am, we're doing just fine,' she'd replied, straightening her apron across her ample bosom. 'You go off and enjoy your party. Everything is under control in here.' She'd smiled at me, her rosy cheeks dimpled as a twinkle had appeared in her soft brown eyes.

'Off you go now and don't worry,' she'd insisted, pushing me out of the kitchen towards the throng of the party.

I'd smiled to myself as I'd headed towards the ballroom. Mrs Brown had been a real asset to the household. I'd been so pleased when she'd agreed to come and run the house for us. She'd always run a tight ship and

I'd trusted her with my life. After all, she had been with me all of my life.

The ballroom, like the banqueting hall, had been decorated with candles and festoons of flowers; roses in subtle shades of white, pink and crimson, their delicate scent filling the room. A string quartet had played at one end of the room and the guests had been dancing, their tinkling laughter ringing out above the waltz.

I'd been awed by the sight before me. Marco had decided on a masquerade ball. Everyone had been dressed in the most exquisite costumes of brightly coloured satin, heavily embroidered brocade and gentle shifts of silk. Hats and feather boas had been everywhere; it had reminded me of a rainbow.

'Do you like it?' a deep husky voice had whispered in my ear, sending goose bumps across my skin. My breath had caught and my stomach had flipped as I'd turned to face him.

'Oh, Marco, it's wonderful. Thank you,' I'd said, gazing up into his sapphire eyes. He'd smiled at me and had taken my hand.

'Would you like to dance, Madam?' he'd said, his dark hair shining in the candlelight.

'Why yes, kind Sir, I would be honoured,' I'd replied, curtseying demurely before collapsing in a fit of giggles.

Pulling me into his arms, Marco had kissed me. His lips had been firm as they'd pressed against mine, igniting a fire deep within me. I'd been breathless as we'd drawn apart and my chest had heaved within the confines of my bodice. As Marco had traced a finger along my swollen lips, I'd closed my eyes and moaned softly.

'You look breath-taking, my love,' Marco had whispered, nuzzling my neck as we'd clung to each other on the dance floor. 'Let's get out of here, shall we, and leave them to enjoy the party without us?'

Nodding, I'd followed him across the dance floor, through the brightly clad mass of bodies, to the hallway and the stairs. My senses had been in overdrive. I'd been aware of my shallow breathing and of the pearl choker around my neck that had felt as if it had been strangling me. I'd been able to hear my skirts rustling as I'd climbed the winding staircase, the nets chaffing my skin, while the ivory satin had glinted in the dappled moonlight.

Marco had closed the bedroom door and had turned towards me. His fingers had been icy against my clammy skin as he'd begun to release me from my ivory cage. My own fingers had fumbled with the buttons of his shirt before I'd ripped it open in frustration and had run my shaky fingers over the contours of his lean body.

'Don't be afraid, my love,' he'd said as he'd carried me

to the four- poster bed and had laid me down on the crisp white sheets. Standing before me, he'd removed the rest of his clothes and my heart had skipped a beat as I'd taken in the details of his body and his desire for me. He'd climbed onto the bed and had lain down next to me, tracing the lines of my body with his fingers, exploring every inch, in a way that had made me cry out for him.

'Your turn now,' he'd said as he'd taken my hand and had guided me in my discovery of his body.

Slowly and gently, Marco had made love to me, taking me through the initial pain to the ecstasy I'd heard so much about.

Sweating and spent, we'd lain wrapped in each other's arms, gazing at the full moon through the open window.

'Beautiful, isn't it?' Marco had whispered and I'd nodded and had nestled deeper into his arms.

'The night is so much calmer and exciting than the daytime, don't you think so, Juliet?'

I'd nodded again, not really listening to him, still tingling from our lovemaking.

'How would you like to share the nights with me, forever?'

'Oh, Marco,' I'd said, 'I am yours now, you know that. All I want is to be with you.'

Turning me around to face him, he'd smiled at me. 'I love you and I want us to be together, forever.'

'So do I, Marco. So do I,' I'd whispered, closing my eyes.

He'd leaned in and had kissed me hard before his lips had traced along my jawline, down to my neck, just below my left ear. A ripple of pleasure had run through me, as longing had flooded my body once again.

Marco's grip had grown tighter and tighter as he'd held me to him. I'd felt as if I'd been suffocating; I just hadn't been able to get the space to get any air in. My heart had begun to pound and alarm signals had been firing in my brain. I'd tried to pull away, but he'd been much too strong. I'd cried out as his teeth had pierced the delicate skin of my throat.

The initial pain had been like a pinprick compared to the fire that had soon torn through my body. I'd pushed against him with all my strength, but I'd just been growing weaker. The longer he'd drawn on me, the less energy I had to fight; to fight the man I'd loved; the man I'd just married; the man who'd been draining my body of life.

When I awoke it had still been dark, but Marco had gone. I'd felt groggy and my neck had throbbed. Pulling myself up into a sitting position, I'd swung my legs off the side of the bed, having immediately regretted it as the room had spun and my stomach had flipped. I'd gripped the sides of the bed to steady myself and had pushed myself up to standing.

Wrapping my robe around me, I'd wobbled towards the bedroom door; the wall being my prop in case the dizziness and nausea had returned. *What had Marco done to me?* The thick oak of the bedroom door had felt like a tonne weight and I'd had to use my bodyweight for resistance in order to open it.

As I had done so, the sound that had assailed my ears had been like nothing I'd ever heard before. It had sounded like I'd always imagined the mythological wailing banshee to have sounded. I'd winced as I'd moved onto the landing, the keening of the guests hurting my eardrums.

Beneath the crying; beneath the screams, I'd thought I'd heard something else – male voices; angry voices. I'd tried to focus as I'd staggered to the top of the stairs, but my vision had been blurring and my head had started to throb.

'Marco, where are you?' I'd whispered and had slumped onto a stair halfway down. I'd rested my head against the wall, the cool stone having acted as a balm against the pounding inside my skull.

'Marco?' I'd said, more loudly. 'Marco, where are you? What's going on?'

'Shhh! Be quiet, Juliet! They'll hear you,' a gruff voice had sounded from the bottom of the stairs.

Stumbling down the last few stairs, I'd been able to see Marco peering into the ballroom through a gap in the doors.

'What's happening?' I'd said as I'd reached his side and he'd hugged me to him. I'd jumped and felt Marco's hand clamp over my mouth as another scream had erupted from the room, followed by the stench of burning flesh.

'Where is he?' one of the intruders had demanded.

'I-I-I d-d-don't k-k-know,' one of the guests had replied.

'Where is he?' the intruder had said again as the sizzling sound of flesh being burned had reached us in the hallway.

'Oh God, Marco, do something!' I'd whispered, horrified by the scene I'd been able to see through the doors. 'What are they here for? Who are they?'

'They are hunters and they're here for me. After all this time, they have finally found me,' he'd said; his voice devoid of emotion as he'd watched through the doors.

'Hunters? What hunters? What are you talking about? You're not making any sense..,' I'd drifted off then, the sentence unfinished, because I'd known – deep down, I'd known - who these men had been. As I'd raised my hand to touch the puncture wounds on my neck, Marco had grabbed my wrist.

'Listen to me, Juliet,' he'd said, fixing me with a stern look. 'You've got to get out of here, tonight.'

'No! I'm not leaving you,' I'd whispered as my eyes had filled with tears.

'Yes you are. I want you to be safe. They don't know

about you and so they won't look for you. Dress quickly and go down the back stairs, at the other side of the bedroom, and out through the kitchen. A horse is waiting for you there. Ride as fast as you can and as far away as you can. I will come and find you.'

'No! I won't leave you. I want to be with you, please,' I'd said, but he'd shaken his head.

'Go, Juliet. I will come and find you as soon as I can.'

'But how…,'

'I just will. I need to know you are safe. Now, please go and remember; I love you.' He'd kissed me on the forehead before he'd swept into the ballroom, leaving me staring after him.

Not wanting to disobey him, I'd run back upstairs and had dressed quickly. I'd crept down the back stairs and out into the yard where my horse had been waiting. Mounting her, as quietly as I could, I'd left and I hadn't turned back; not until I'd reached the shelter of the forest.

There I'd stopped and, taking a deep breath, I'd turned around. The whole house had been ablaze. People had been fleeing, alight with flames, only to be killed by the men on horseback, who'd been waiting in the grounds. The cries of the dying and the wounded had rolled towards me through the night air. Tears had flowed down my cheeks as I'd sat and watched friends and relatives killed;

slaughtered; all because they'd known Marco.

I'd sat there for what seemed like hours, hoping to see him come riding out of the carnage, but he never had. Finally, I'd decided to keep going. I had to; before the hunters had left the scene. I'd needed to distance myself from there, just as Marco had said, and then wait for him to come and find me.

He'd promised he would find me and I had known that I'd wait for him. No matter how long he'd take, I would wait.

I opened my eyes, fresh tears having dampened my cheeks at the memories. I had waited for him; waited for over a hundred years, but he never came. I gave up hoping a long time ago, but there was always that little part of me that hung on.

He'd been the love of my life; my only love. I looked around me at this broken shell that had once symbolised the start of my life with Marco.

He hadn't survived the fire, I was sure of that now, but I could still feel him in this place. I could feel his touch on my skin and could feel my body begin to respond. Shuddering, I turned to leave, my heart heavy.

'Juliet my love, don't leave,' his voice echoed through this carcass and as I turned, I swear I could see a figure in the shadows.

'Marco?' I said and started towards it.

'Juliet, where did you go? I couldn't find you,' his voice continued to echo through the space.

'For goodness sake, Juliet, have you lost your mind? He's gone; forget it; just leave,' I chastised myself and closed my eyes. Opening them again, I stared ahead of me at the blackened stone wall. There was no one there now; he was gone.

'Goodbye, Marco,' I said as I turned and walked away, dousing the embers forever.

THE END

11 THE CREATURE WITHIN

John's eyes were wild. He could feel the panic escalating through his body; could hear his heart hammering against his rib cage.

'Must go faster, must go faster,' he chanted, as he pumped his legs faster and faster, his breathing becoming shallower as he gulped the chill night air into his screaming lungs.

What the hell had possessed him to come running in the park? Why couldn't he just train with the team like everyone else did? He shuddered, angry with himself. His stupid ego, that's why. Before the accident, he had been the best basketball player the college team had and now look at him; struggling to run a couple of miles through the park. John could see the row of houses on the other side of the railings, lit up like lighthouses against the intense blackness of the night.

'C'mon, dammit, faster,' he urged himself, wishing he was in the midst of another one of his parents' arguments; wishing he was anywhere, but here.

He stumbled on the uneven ground, his left ankle

giving out under the strain.

'Noooooo!' he screamed, throwing out his arms to try to break his fall. John hit the ground hard; the pain in his newly mended ankle shooting warning signals to his brain.

'Got to get up, got to get up. Nearly there, nearly home,' he muttered, drifting in and out of consciousness; the pain from his ankle causing waves of nausea to wrack his body.

Just then he heard it. Lucidity returned. Panic began to overwhelm him again, flooding his limbs with the adrenalin he needed. Pushing himself up, he bit down on his lip and winced as he leaned on his damaged ankle. The pain was excruciating, but he had to move; he had no choice. The gap in the railings wasn't far and then he would be home.

John heard it again; the unearthly howling that had plagued him during his run through the park. At first, he had thought it was one of the animals from Chekov's Circus, but he had passed their cages a while back and the howling was just as clear now as it had been back then. Something was following him; he was sure of it. He couldn't see anything, but the hairs on the back of his neck had been on alert for a while and goose bumps were running rampant across his skin. Something was definitely watching him.

Limping as fast as he could across the uneven ground, he tried to locate the gap in the railings; the gap that had been there since he was at primary school; the gap they had all sneaked through into the park after closing time; the gap that was going to save his life. Terror replaced panic as his wild eyes faced a solid line of railings; eight feet high and topped with barbed wire. Disbelieving, he scoured the length of metal, but did not locate any defects. John dropped to his knees in despair, a sob escaping his throat as he realised his predicament.

The creature was getting closer now, having stalked its prey through the park. It was time to move in for the kill. It had tracked him ever since he'd entered the park; his fluorescent covering making him an easy target, without the unbearable stench that humans gave off. He had been too easy a target, almost not worth the effort, but not quite.

It waited in the cover of the trees, watching him slumped over on all fours, his body heaving. It ran a long purple tongue over its razor sharp teeth and, pointing its nose towards the sky, let out a blood-curdling howl. It was time.

John started at the noise and looked around him. He couldn't see anything in the pitch dark. He could hear the trees rustling in the wind and, as he strained to make out other sounds, he heard the rasping breaths. He squeezed his eyes shut tight, forcing tears to seep out from under his eyelids. He could hear footsteps now; heavy and even. They were circling him. John didn't want to open his eyes; he didn't want to see what was stalking him. He felt the creature draw closer to him. He could smell the dampness of its skin; he could smell the death and decay on its breath; he could feel the warmth of its breath and the wetness of its nose as it stood face to face with him.

Keeping his eyes firmly shut, John kept as still as he could, hoping the creature would think him already dead and go away. As if hearing his prayer, the creature did move away from him. Too elated to think straight, John opened his eyes, just in time to see the creature as it lunged for him. Its talon like claws ripped open his abdomen and he felt the contents of his lower body emptying out onto the grass. As the darkness drew in on him, he saw the creature's fangs as it lunged for his neck, tearing his throat wide open.

The creature, full and sated, sloped back into the cover of the trees. As it disappeared, the moon emerged from behind the clouds, as though it had been hiding, and illuminated the carnage in an eerie green glow. It was a full moon.

The young man lay six feet from the railings, spread-eagled on the grass, his vacant stare reflecting the glow of the moon. His body was turned inside out; his fingers twitching as his life ebbed away. Why did he go running in the park? The question was imprinted in his glassy stare forever.

The wind picked up and as the branches from a young sapling rose and fell on the current, the gap in the railings came into view.

Ellie awoke as the morning sunshine began to warm her naked body. She stretched and rolled over, feeling for Brad on the grass next to her. *Already gone*, she mused, *what a chicken*. She sat up and looked towards the back of her parent's house. Their curtains were still drawn, which was a good sign. They would not be impressed if they found her like this. She giggled to herself as she scrabbled around for the clothes she had been wearing the previous night. Where on earth had she put them? She sat up and looked around, shielding her eyes from the harsh light of the dawning sun.

Where the hell were her clothes? *Brad must have taken them*, she thought. She'd get him back. She jumped up and headed for the back door. Luckily, her parents still believed her when she said she wouldn't be home late and had left the door unlocked. She closed it behind her and listened for any movements from upstairs. Nothing. As quickly as she could, Ellie scampered upstairs into the safety of her room, collapsing onto the bed; her heart pounding.

She smiled to herself as she thought about the previous night. Brad was such a thoughtful lover; and wild. Her body still tingled from what he had done to her. Afterwards, they had smoked some pot, or rather a lot of pot, and then things had become a bit hazy. What had happened after that?

Shrugging her slender shoulders, Ellie padded into her bathroom and looked at herself in the mirror. *Something must have happened*, she mused as she plucked leaves out of her thick wavy hair, *because these certainly didn't grow in her father's garden*.

Humming to herself, she perched on the edge of the bath and turned on the taps. She poured in a capful of her favourite jasmine scented bath oil and began swirling the now cloudy water. Her thoughts returned to Brad; all six feet four inches of dark good looks and mystery. As usual, her father hadn't been impressed.

'He's a mechanic, Ellie,' her father had said. 'What future can he possibly give you? Why isn't he at University with other kids his age?'

Who cares, thought Ellie, her mind full of the previous night and of Brad's strong arms and toned torso and…

'Arghhh!' Ellie screamed and doubled over in pain as

the first wave of cramps overtook her body. She hit the floor, with a thud, as she fainted; the sound of the running water fading away as she slipped into darkness.

Barbara Parker awoke with a start as she heard her daughter's screams. She jumped out of bed, knocking Nostradamus from his comfy perch. The grey cat growled in disgust and stalked out of the room, as Barbara raced into her daughter's room.

'Ellie, where are you, sweetheart?'

Pushing open the bathroom door, she saw Ellie slumped on the floor; her athletic body convulsing as the waves of cramps surged through her.

'Oh my God.' Barbara turned off the taps and, grabbing a towel, she dropped to the floor and wrapped it around her daughter. Hugging Ellie to her, Barbara began to rock her back and forth, whispering her name, urging her to come round. As tears coursed down her pale cheeks, she absently traced the jagged scar on her daughter's limp left forearm. Barbara leant her head back against the bath, a lock of her dark hair falling across her face, and closed her eyes.

'Bar, what's going on?' Jack asked as he rubbed his eyes, trying his best to wake up.

'What does it look like, Jack?' she said, 'it's that time of the month again and look at her.' A sob escaped her throat as her green eyes rested on her unconscious daughter.

'There's nothing we can do, Bar. The doctors have said it is just her body's way of dealing with it.'

'Jack, there is nothing natural about the onset of her period. I mean, look at her. This is not what should happen.'

'I know, honey, but what else can we do?'

Jack left the question hanging in the air as he went downstairs to start his day with coffee and the Saturday financial press.

Barbara felt Ellie flinch and realised she had been taking her annoyance with her husband out on Ellie's scar, which was now red raw. That was odd. After all these years, it shouldn't still hurt her. Barbara thought back to the day Ellie got the scar.

They had had an Alsatian, Greco, who Ellie had been nursing back to health after he had been attacked by a wild animal. The dog had been really sick and Ellie had been insistent that he should stay with her while he recovered. One night while she slept, the dog had turned on her and had torn a chunk out of her arm. Jack had had to subdue Greco with a baseball bat and they'd had to have him put down. Ellie had never really gotten over it.

'That's why we decided to get you, isn't it, Damus?' Barbara said to the cat sitting in the bathroom doorway, his orange eyes fixed firmly on Ellie's inert body.

At the sound of her mother's voice, Ellie began to stir and the cat, hackles raised, started hissing and spitting at her.

'Damus! What is wrong with you? Get out of here,' Barbara shooed him away as she helped Ellie to sit up.

'How are you feeling, baby?' Barbara said, as she swept a lock of sand coloured hair behind Ellie's ear.

'Like I've been run over by a train,' Ellie said, managing a small smile. 'I think I'll salvage my bath and soak in it for a while.'

'Okay, sweetie. I'll go and start breakfast.'

As Barbara left the bathroom, Ellie hauled herself back up onto the side of the bath and turned the hot tap back on. Nostradamus sat watching her from the doorway.

'Come here, Damus,' Ellie said. Damus just hissed at her and disappeared.

'Stupid cat,' she muttered. What was wrong with him just lately?

Too exhausted to care, she slipped into the exotic scented steam, gritting her teeth against the hot pokers now stabbing every part of her body. Submerged up to her neck in the oil-laden water, she rested her head against the soft pillow that spent its life suctioned to one end of the bath. She began to relax as the hot water worked its magic; soothing the pains away. Ellie closed her eyes and let herself drift away.

She was with Brad. They were holding hands and laughing together as they strolled through the park. The moon was full, but the night was cloudy and so they walked mainly in darkness. Brad began walking faster and faster, dragging her behind him, until they were running flat out. He pulled her through the trees, her long hair snagging on the low branches. She wasn't laughing anymore; she was crying. Brad looked back at her and grinned, before letting go of her hand and racing off into the woods. She stood, frozen to the spot, as she heard the blood-curdling howl and saw the flash of white teeth and blood red eyes.

Ellie awoke with a start, her heart pounding. Where the hell had that come from? She shivered, not sure whether it was because of the dream or because the water had cooled considerably. Climbing out of the bath, she wrapped herself in a thick fluffy towel.

She padded back into her bedroom and sat down at her dressing table and looked at herself in the mirror. The cramps had certainly taken their toll. Her sapphire eyes lacked their usual shine and her rosy cheeks looked grey and hollow. As she picked up her hairbrush, Ellie could hear her parents downstairs, talking about her. They weren't shouting, they were just talking, but she could hear them clearly.

'There's something wrong with her, Jack. There must be.'

'Oh, for God's sake, Bar, I'm not going over this again. We're just going to have to live with it. The doctors said it would get easier for her as she gets older. They said it's always harder for late developers and, let's face it, she was seventeen before any of this started.'

'I know that, Jack, and she's only eighteen now. What's she going to be like in ten years? These episodes are getting worse and the blackouts longer. She's changing, Jack. She's not the Ellie she used to be – she's moody; she's erratic; she's aggressive .... and even Damus doesn't seem too fond of her anymore. They used to be inseparable.'

'Come on, Barbara, she's growing up, that's all. As for Damus; he's just jealous of Brad. He's only been acting odd since she started seeing him,' Jack said.

'Yes, but that's not all. That scar on Ellie's arm; it's all raw again and she flinched when I touched it.'

'Honey, that's just psychological. Greco meant a lot to her.'

'She was unconscious at the time.'

Unsure of what else to say, Jack returned to his newspaper.

Damus, who was munching happily on his breakfast, hissed as Ellie entered the kitchen and disappeared through his cat flap into the garden.

Ellie was dressed in jeans, a white T-shirt and trainers;

her sandy coloured hair pulled back in a ponytail. She had carefully applied her makeup to disguise her pallor, so as not to worry her parents.

'I'm going to Brad's,' she said, as she plucked a piece of toast from the pile on the table.

'Aren't you going to have a proper breakfast first, sweetie? It'll make you feel better,' Barbara said.

'I'm okay, Mum. I'll get something later.'

'Are you sure you should be going out to see him after what happened this morning? Maybe you should go and lie down for a while.'

'Maybe you should mind your own damn business,' Ellie snarled, her white teeth flashing in the sunlight.

'Eleanor Parker, don't you...,' Jack started to say, but she was gone.

What the hell was wrong with her? Ellie wondered as she jogged away from her house before her father followed her, slowing to a walk at the end of her street. She scratched her left arm and winced. Looking down she saw her ten-year old scar as raw as the day she was stitched up and sore as hell. A growl erupted from inside her as she touched the wound. Startled, she looked around her, wondering where it had come from, but she was alone in the street. Puzzled, she shrugged her shoulders and headed towards Brad's.

It was about eleven o'clock when she got there and, standing on the doorstep in the midst of the overgrown garden, she knocked on the green front door; the paint flaking off under the pressure of her knuckles. She waited for five minutes, knowing Brad's mum, Jan, would have heard her and would be pulling her dressing gown on, annoyed at having her sleep interrupted. Jan worked two jobs and still earned barely enough to feed her three kids. Brad helped out, but Jan wanted him to start saving for a place of his own; for a future.

'Hey, Ellie,' Jan said as she opened the door, wincing at the brightness of the sunshine.

'Hi, Jan. I'm sorry to wake you. Is Brad in?' Ellie said, feeling guilty for having deprived Jan of some well needed rest.

'I'm sorry, El, but he's gone to one of his Biker Meets'. Didn't he tell you? I thought he always told you,' Jan said, trying her best to stifle a yawn.

'Yeah, he usually does,' Ellie said. 'Due back Monday, isn't he?'

'Yep. Look, I don't mean to be rude, but I need to get some sleep. I'm on at two. I'll see you soon, El.' With that, she closed the door.

'Yeah, bye,' Ellie muttered to the closed door.

Bloody motorbikes, Ellie thought. *Why hadn't he told her?* As she kicked the gatepost on her way out, a chunk of concrete broke away at the force, but she didn't notice.

Brad had been a member of a biker gang, The Vipers, ever since he was sixteen. They went away every month for a few days to these meets, which were held at various places around the country.

'We just talk about bikes and stuff,' he'd said, when she'd asked about them.

Why then, if that's all they did, did new members have to go through an initiation ceremony; wrestling wild dogs and drinking animal blood? Ellie wondered; not for the first time.

It bothered her that he hadn't told her he was going, or maybe he had, but she had been too stoned to remember. That was it; it had to be. With her black mood starting to lift, Ellie stopped and took stock of her surroundings. She was outside the park.

Curious as to why she had walked here; she decided to carry on into the park. *Why had she come here?* Maybe she and Brad had arranged to meet here. But why, when he knew he was going away? Tired and disappointed at not being able to see Brad, Ellie found a sheltered spot of grass, out of sight from the path, and sat down. Staring intently into the undergrowth, Ellie swore something was looking back at her. She shook her head, chastising herself for her paranoia, and lay back. As the midday sun warmed her body, she drifted off to sleep.

When she awoke, she was disorientated and it took a few minutes for her to remember where she was. It was dusk now, Ellie shivered as the cool evening breeze caused goose bumps to pattern her bare arms. Rubbing her hands up and down her arms to warm them up, Ellie sat up and stretched, looking at her watch. It was seven thirty. God, she must have been tired.

Ellie stood up, deciding to go for a walk before she went home. She and Brad came to the park quite a lot. They liked to watch the sun go down over the lake and this was where she headed.

She walked along the slatted jetty to the end and stared out across the lake. The sky was a burnt orange; the final glow of the setting sun lighting the horizon up like fire. The warmth of the air cooled as it touched the lake, creating a mist that hovered just above the surface.

With the orange sky fading fast to pale yellow, Ellie sat down cross-legged on the edge of the jetty to watch the final lights of the day fade away. She closed her eyes and leaned back on her elbows, allowing the evening breeze to caress her skin; soothing her. She turned her face, to capture the last tendrils of sunlight, and picked up his scent. Goose bumps erupted across her flesh once again. She lay back and stretched her arms over her head, reaching towards him.

She felt the boards of the jetty vibrate under his weight, as he made his way towards her, and she smiled; wicked thoughts jumping into her mind. *No one was around; no one would see them*, she thought, and shuddered, as a ripple of pleasure suffused her abdomen.

She started to peel off her clothes, desire flooding her body as she thought of him; thought of them, the previous night. As her mind replayed events, her fingers began to trace the curves of her body; her nails, now elongated and sharp, tearing trails through her flesh as she did so.

She could feel him drawing near her; she could hear his heavy rasping breath. Ellie growled with pleasure. His cool nose touched her face and she opened her eyes and looked straight into blood red ones. Ellie jumped and tried to scream, but all that emerged was a deep guttural growl. Terrified, she scrambled over onto all fours and tried to stand up, but she couldn't; her spine wouldn't allow it. As she struggled to stand, tears brimming her eyes, she fell back on her haunches and found herself face to face with it.

The creature took a step towards her, but she shrank away; her eyes wild and afraid. It continued to move towards her, its red eyes shining and its jet-black fur almost silvery in the glow from the newly risen moon. Panicked, Ellie jumped as far as she could into the lake and swam towards the shore. Hauling herself up onto the bank, she turned and looked back at the jetty, but the creature was gone.

Afraid it was coming for her, she again tried to stand up, but couldn't. She finally looked down and, in the light cast by the moon, Ellie stared in horror at the thick golden fur that covered her. Terrified, she clawed at her body, desperate to rid herself of it, but she only succeeded in cutting herself with her sharp claws. The rich smell of blood invaded her nostrils and awoke her senses. She felt her stomach rumble and her mouth begin to water; her hunger suddenly urgent and intoxicating.

Ellie stared at the wounds on her stomach and, to her disgust, felt herself start to lick them clean. Suddenly, she froze; the creature had found her. She could sense it. The familiar smell; the scent that she thought only Brad carried. She wheeled around and stared at the creature before her. Her eyes blazing and her teeth bared, Ellie launched herself towards it, but changed direction at the last minute and disappeared into the trees.

She didn't look back this time, she just ran, tears streaming through the damp fur of her face. She ran as fast as she could; she didn't know where, she just ran. Her breath was rasping now; her lungs screaming, but she didn't care. All she could think about was getting as far away from it as possible.

All of a sudden, the ground vanished from beneath her

feet and she felt herself falling. She reached out to grab anything that would break her fall, but there was nothing within reach. She hit the ground with a thud. As Ellie lost consciousness, she caught sight of a pair of red eyes looking down at her from the top of the slope she had just fallen down.

Ellie screwed her eyes up tight against the glaring sunlight and, shielding them, she tried to sit up, but the pain shooting through her head forced her to lie back down.

'Ohhh,' she groaned.

'Ellie, are you all right?'

'Brad, is that you? What are you doing here? I thought you were away. Where am I? Where are my clothes? Brad… What the hell is going on?' Ellie started to sob; her headache making her feel sick.

'You don't remember what happened last night?' Brad said, running his fingers through her hair.

'No, it must have been all that weed you gave me,' Ellie said, trying to sit up. She winced at the stabbing pains in her head and groped around for her clothes.

'That wasn't last night, El. That was the night before. You were in the park last night. You're still in the park. You fell. Don't you remember?' He handed her the clothes he had retrieved from the jetty and she quickly put them on.

'What are you talking about?' she said, turning to face him.

'Come on, El, you must remember. You were on the jetty, naked, waiting for me, or at least I hope you were waiting for me. But when you saw me, you took off.'

'What…I don't…oh my God,' Ellie said and stared at him in horror. 'That was you? But I thought I had dreamt it, especially me, covered in fur and…' Ellie tailed off as she stared into his eyes. They were the same eyes she had looked into last night, except they were tawny now, not red. She started to cry and Brad sat down next to her and hugged her to him; his raven head bent against her sandy one.

'But I don't understand…' she sobbed, her mind reeling as she tried to make sense out of it all. 'I didn't think creatures like that actually existed, Brad. I've heard the tales, but I thought…'

'I know, baby, I know,' Brad said, kissing her hair.

'But how, Brad? You….me….how?'

'Deep down, I think you know about me. The Vipers, the initiation – they were werewolves. They were the people who befriended me and they were different. We go away for a few days around the full moon, as far away from our families as we can.'

'But why not this time?'

'Because of you. I knew you were one of us, El; I could feel it. Then you told me about Greco and it all fell into place.'

'Then why has it taken so long? Why wasn't I a. …werewolf when it happened?'

'You don't change until you reach maturity. For you, it only happened recently. Haven't you noticed yourself changing, El?'

Ellie sat there, her head resting against Brad's chest, his arms wrapped around her; protecting her; making her feel safe. She stared out over the mass of trees spread out around them and listened to the birds singing; to the animals scurrying around in the undergrowth; and to the conversations going on elsewhere in the park; conversations she wouldn't have been able to hear a few short months ago.

It all made sense now, in a weird kind of way. Her erratic behaviour; her amazing hearing; the soreness of her scar; and, most of all, Damus' change in behaviour towards her. She shook her head in disbelief.

'Are you okay?' Brad said, his voice tinged with concern.

'I just don't know what to say. I mean, what happens now? What do I tell my parents?' Ellie said, a sob catching in her throat.

'Hey, hey, don't cry, baby, don't cry. I'll look after you.'

Ellie closed her eyes and tried to believe in Brad. What choice did she have? He was the only one who understood her now.

They stayed like that all afternoon; each lost in their own thoughts; each waiting for something. As the sun began to set, ready for the last full moon of the cycle, Ellie could feel her body changing. Her fear had been replaced with amazement, as she watched the golden fur spread across her body; as she watched her nails elongate and curl into the talons she had stared at in horror the night before. She caught her breath as her body was flung forward and her spine arched, forcing her onto all fours. As she felt her teeth growing and her face changing shape, she stared up at the moon.

Ellie watched as Brad disappeared into the trees, but she didn't follow; not yet. She sat still for a while, the moonlight glinting off the golden fur that now covered her body. She looked down at the talons that were her nails and raising her long snout to the moon, she let out a howl that would make your blood run cold. She then loped after Brad.

On the other side of the park, a young couple started at the sound. They sat still; listening intently.

'It's just one of the circus animals,' Paul said to Emma. 'Come on, relax.'

Emma started to giggle as he tickled her and they fell back into the grass.

A short distance away, in the darkness of the trees; two pairs of red eyes watched; and two purple tongues ran along two sets of razor sharp fangs. The hunt was on, but tonight he wouldn't be alone.

THE END

12 THE NIGHT STALKER

It is November and the nights have well and truly drawn in now; the red and gold glows of autumn having given way gracefully to the throws of winter. The trees, now stripped of their beauty, shiver as the wind bites through their barren branches, ripping the last of their dignity from them. The driving rain batters the cracked pavements, while the wounded call of the wind carries along the deserted streets.

Jet black eyes scan the street, focusing in on the sound. He raises his head slightly, his aquiline nose picking up the scent. Clinging to the shadows, he creeps forward, without a sound, never taking his eyes off his prey.

Then, as if pausing for breath, the wind drops and the rain slows to a dull pattering. Silence envelopes the scene. The streets are calm; the elements exhausted. Nothing moves. Nothing makes a sound; well, barely.

The clouds begin parting company to reveal the greenish glow of a new moon, casting the street in a dappled half-light. He dives into a doorway, chest heaving, but it is too late; he has been seen. His shoulders sag in defeat as he watches his quarry scurry away.

'Please, not another night like the last one,' he mutters, 'I just don't have the strength.'

It is his own fault; he has left it too long between feeds; left it until it is almost too late. He hates hunting, he always has, but it is the only way he can survive; the only way he can sustain his pitiful existence.

Tuesday night was a night like this one, except the wind and the rain were pounding the town into submission. At least the moon had kept its distance; giving him a fighting chance. He pulled his scarf around his face to keep out the rain, while the icy wind gnawed at his bare hands and dragged at his heavy coat. The wind didn't bother him; it never had; it never would. Why? Because he couldn't feel it. The rain, however, was a different matter. It got in his way; it affected his co-ordination and that was dangerous.

As if sensing his annoyance, the rain slowed and he lowered his scarf, tucking it inside his coat. He hated nights like this; nights when he had to keep moving, so his senses wouldn't become affected by the monotonous drone of rain; so he would not mistake the sound for something more important. He longed for a dry night; a night when he could hide and listen for what he wanted; for what he needed. Even the snow, with its blanket of silence, was better than this interminable racket.

As if on cue, the pounding started again and he swore under his breath. He began walking, like he did every night; listening and waiting. He was hungry and if he didn't get something soon, he would be in trouble; he knew that.

A door banged open across the street and loud rock music rolled towards him through the veil of rain. The music intensified the pounding, which seemed to surround him; drawing him in; engulfing him; injecting its beat into him until he felt it pulsate in his veins.

'Dammit!' he said, as his head began to throb; his senses disorientated. He was not having a good night.

Swarms of young people burst out into the street as the club emptied its contents for the night. He heard them, screaming and shouting; jostling and fighting. He was getting weaker and knew he had to make his move soon. He watched as they split into groups and went their separate ways. He followed as they drifted away and as he rounded a corner he saw a small group of girls, huddled under one umbrella. He drew back into the shadows to watch; to plan.

'I'll ring my dad, he'll come and get us,' a tall skinny redhead said.

'And let him know where we've been? Yeah, great idea,' another, whom he couldn't see, snorted.

'No, I won't tell him. I'll just say to pick us up someplace else.'

'And just tell me where, in this awful place, could we tell him to meet us?'

'But I just want to go home. I don't feel too good,' the redhead continued.

He watched as the other two walked off, leaving the redhead to trail behind. He followed them, so close he could taste the alcohol on their breath, as they laughed and joked about their illicit night out.

They never heard a thing.

He shudders as he remembers that night. He hates doing that, but his instincts took over and he was powerless to stop. He swore that he would not let it happen again; that he would not let himself go so long between feeds. To do that, though, he would have to find a way to accept his fate; he would have to find a way to manage his fate.

Resigned to another barren night, he leaves the shadows. The moonlight casts his face in a luminescent glow; his hollow cheeks dark in the half-light; his thick heavy brows, shadowing his eyes. He rakes a translucent, bony hand through his raven hair; the tracks visible in the shoulder length mane. His brows furrow and he purses his crimson lips as he wonders, once again, how he has ended up like this. How had he let this happen to him?

'How indeed,' he says, leaning against a wall and resting his head against its cool damp skin. He shudders as he remembers his sire; remembers his transformation. Why had he let it happen? He'd had no choice. If he hadn't, he would have died. His father had been gravely ill and there had been no one else to take care of him. He couldn't have just left him to die; he'd loved him too much for that. His father had died the next day.

Not wanting his friends to see the monster he'd become, he'd left the village and had spent his time on the move. He'd never stayed too long in one place, for fear that he would be discovered.

That is how he'd existed for the past 248 years; for existing is all it had been.

Although he knows what he is, he loathes it and rarely feeds on humans, unless he is desperate. Sometimes the pain gets too much to bear and he has to give in to what he really is. What happened the other night was a mistake; a nightmare he knows will never go away.

He can't believe how quickly they found her. Someone must have seen him; there is no other way she could have been found so quickly. He has to be more careful. He can't afford to let that happen again; can't afford to let himself get so weak. He has to survive, but there is only one way he can survive. He gags at the thought and slides down the wall to the ground. What is he going to do; he is so hungry?

Just then he hears a scream and, jumping to his feet, heads towards it. As he rounds a bend, he sees a young woman being attacked by what appears to be an old man. His face changes as the monster within him takes over; the adrenalin flowing into his muscles, renewing the strength he is rapidly losing. He reaches the pair in an instant and hurls the old man to the ground. Jumping to his feet, the old man lets out a roar and launches himself at his assailant; his claws ripping his opponent's left cheek open like tissue paper.

He can feel the blood running down his face and dripping onto his clothes. Summoning all his strength, he lunges at the old man, his razor like nails slashing through the man's throat. The old man clasps both hands to his neck, a look of shock in his watery eyes, and stumbles away into an alley nearby.

He turns towards the young woman and sees the injuries on her neck.

The wound is open; raw. The flesh glistening with the freshness of her blood. The scent is intoxicating and his gaze remains fixed on the puncture marks; laid bare for him; calling for him; drawing him in.

He approaches her, her heartbeat pounding through his veins; his taste buds electrified; his hunger beyond redemption.

His brain screams at him to turn away; to let her go. His brain reminds him of his vow. His brain reminds him of the other night; of his promise. But his hunger, oh his hunger is so much stronger than his willpower. His hunger is what reminds him that he has to feed. His hunger is what reminds him that he has to survive. His hunger knows just what will make the pain go away.

'But it didn't go away,' he says, closing his eyes and forcing himself to turn away from her; to turn away from the addictive scent. He has to get away; he has to leave. If he doesn't...

'Help me,' the girl whispers and the sound freezes him in his tracks. He knows that voice. He hears it every day as she laughs and jokes with her classmates, while he sits and watches; waiting for the right time.

'No!' he shouts and rushes to her side, grabbing her chin and turning her face towards him, causing her to groan at the ferocity of his grip.

It is her. Her hair, though matted and tangled, is the colour of straw and hangs down her back in thick waves. Her eyes, which he knows are the colour of the sea, are closed now, their spacing on either side of her small upturned nose, giving her a bewitching look; the very look he had fallen for when she'd first walked into his class six months ago.

'Help me,' she mutters again and her eyes flutter. He panics, not wanting her to see him; to recognise him. It isn't time.

'Shhh,' he says, as he feels for her pulse – thin; thready. She's lost too much blood.

'Dammit!' he says and punches the wall behind him; the stonework crumbling beneath his fist. It is too soon. She isn't ready. But, if he doesn't, then she will die. Then he will never get the chance.

He bites his wrist, tearing open the flesh, and then he pushes it to her lips, angling it so the blood runs into her mouth. Once she tastes it, her survival instincts will kick in; they always do.

As if on cue, she begins to draw on him and he braces himself. He has to be careful. He doesn't have much; he needs to feed. He can feel his body getting weaker as she drinks and he only just manages to pull away from her; only just manages to summon the strength. She sighs and her head lolls to one side. He leans back against the wall for support; to steady the dizziness and nausea that now threaten to consume him. He casts a sideways look at her and sees that the wounds on her neck are starting to heal.

It's working, he thinks and closes his eyes for a moment, to let himself recover.

His eyes snap open; his senses alert. He fell asleep. How stupid. Now dawn is approaching. Soon, he will be out of options. He has to move now. He hauls himself to his feet and bends to pick up the woman. As he does so, blood drips onto her blouse and fans out across the thin fabric. The wound on his cheek still hasn't healed.

He heaves her into his arms and her head rests against his shoulder, her scent wafting into his nostrils, making him shudder. He starts to run.

He prays she doesn't wake up; doesn't see him; doesn't recognise him. For, she cannot know his secret. Not yet.

As he lays her down on her front doorstep, she stirs and he freezes. Without opening her eyes, she reaches out and touches the gash on his cheek.

'Thank you,' she says and drifts away again.

He relaxes. That was too close. He reaches out to ring the doorbell and then merges back into the breaking dawn, his ears tuned back into the creatures of the night; his salvation.

THE END

ABOUT THE AUTHOR

In February 2005, Marie Anne Cope had her first short story - Three Silver Bullets - published in Thirteen magazine. Her second publishing credit was seen on the website of Climb magazine in November 2007, for her short story Sheer Hell. Both of these stories have been included in the first volume of Tales From a Scarygirl and have already been read and enjoyed by thousands of people across the world.

In February 2013, Marie published her debut novel - Bonds - followed by the sequel - Broken Bonds - in 2015. The third instalment - Bonds Re-Bound - is currently being penned.

In addition to being a writer, Marie is also a self-employed Accountant and a yoga teacher. She lives in an North Wales with her three cats.

Why not follow Marie at the addresses below:

FB: @MarieAnneCopeAuthor

T: @MarieAnneCope

www.marieannecope.com

Made in the USA
Columbia, SC
02 October 2017